GCSE CHEMISTRY

FLASH NOTES

AQA Higher Tier

New Syllabus 2016 (Grade 9-1)

Dr C. Boes

Condensed Revision Notes (Flashcards) for a Successful Exam Preparation

Designed to Facilitate Memorization

For corrections, comments and special offers go to:
www.alevelchemistryrevision.co.uk

Text copyright © 2018 Dr. Christoph Boes

All rights reserved

Cover Image copyright © Pedro Antonio Salaverría Calahorra
Dreamstime.com (Image ID: 38478674)
http://www.dreamstime.com/pedro2009_info

All other Images copyright © 2016 Dr. Christoph Boes

Self-published 2018

ISBN-13: 978-0-9957060-8-8

Contents

Paper 1 (8462) 7

Topic 1 – Atomic Structure and the Periodic Table 7
Basic Definitions 7
Atomic Models & Electronic Structure 9
Periodic Table 11
Group 1 Alkali Metals 13
Group 7 Halogens & Group 0 Noble Gases 15
Collecting Data 17
Separation Techniques 19
Simple Distillation & Fractional Distillation 21

Topic 2 – Bonding, Structure and Properties of Matter 23
Ionic and Covalent Compounds and Bonds 23
Giant Covalent Structures & Metallic Bonding 25
States of Matter 27
Nanoparticles 29

Topic 3 – Quantitative Chemistry 31
Mole & Molar Gas Volume 31
Calculate Masses & Work out Reaction Equation 33
Percentage Mass & Percentage Yield 35
Atom Economy & Concentrations 37

Topic 4 – Chemical Changes 39
Acids and Bases 39
pH & Titrations 41
List of Anions & Naming Salts & Making Soluble Salts 43
Redox Reactions & Displacement Reaction 45
Balancing Redox Equations & Conservation of Mass 47
Metals and their Reactivity & Extraction of Metals from Ores 49
Electrolysis & Alternative Copper Extractions 51
Aluminium Electrolysis & Sodium Chloride Electrolysis 53
Two Main Types of Inorganic Reactions & Ionic Equations 55

Topic 5 – Energy Changes 57
Electrochemical Cells & Cell Types 57
Exothermic/Endothermic & Bond Energies & Calorimeter 59
Reaction Profiles 61

Paper 2 (8462) 63

Topic 6 – The Rate and Extent of Chemical Change 63
    Rates of Reactions & Catalyst 63
    Measuring Rates of Reaction 65
    Calculating Rates of Reaction 67
    Equilibrium and Reversible Reactions 69

Topic 7 – Organic Chemistry 71
    Alkanes 71
    Crude Oil – Fuel 73
    Alkenes 75
    Addition Polymers & Functional Groups 77
    Alcohols 79
    Carboxylic Acids 81
    Condensation Polymers 83

Topic 8 – Chemical Analysis 85
    Purity and Formulations & Chromatography 85
    Tests for Gases & Tests for Anions 87
    Tests for Cations & Flame Emission Spectroscopy 89

Topic 9 – Chemistry of the Atmosphere 91
    The Atmosphere 91
    The Greenhouse Effect 93

Topic 10 – Using Resources 95
    Materials and their Properties 95
    Metals & Corrosion 97
    Finite and Renewable Resources & Reuse and Recycling 99
    Potable Water 101
    The Haber Process & NPK Fertilisers 103

Appendix: Periodic Table of Elements 105

How to use these notes

Revision notes (revision cards) are an effective and successful way to prepare for exams. They contain the necessary exam knowledge in a condensed, easy to memorize form. These notes are designed for the final stage of revision and require a thorough understanding of the topics. If this understanding is lacking then help from a professional tutor and additional studies of text books or revision guides is suggested.

These revision notes are organized in chapters according to the current AQA GCSE Higher Tier specification 8462 (from Sept 2016). Each chapter contains individual revision cards covering all the necessary topics. Everything in *italic* is optional knowledge, aimed at students who want to excel or want to continue to A-Level. **Bold** represents important keywords or key definitions. *'Given'* indicates information which will be provided in the exam questions and does not need to be memorized. Important information and exam-specific tips are highlighted in yellow.

How to memorize: The revision cards are introduced by their titles and keywords on a separate page. After reading the title you should try to write down the content of the card without looking at the next page. The keywords give you hints about the content. Write down everything you remember, even if you are not sure. Then check if your answers are correct; if not, rewrite the incorrect ones.

At the beginning, when you are still unfamiliar with the cards, it might help to read them a few times first. If they contain a lot of content, you can cover the revision card with a piece of paper and slowly reveal the header and sub content. While you uncover it try to remember what is written in the covered part, e.g. the definition for a term you just uncovered. This uncovering technique is for the early stages, later you should be able to write down the whole content after just reading the header. If this is the case, move to the next card. If not, bookmark the card and memorize it repeatedly. Do at least four to five sessions per week until you know all the cards of one chapter word-perfectly. When you have memorized a revision card apply your new knowledge by answering topic questions. Then move on to the next section. Generally it is better to do shorter sessions more often than longer sessions less frequently. An even better option is to ask somebody to check your knowledge by reading the header aloud and comparing your answer to the content.

Exam techniques

Begin with a quick look through the exam. How is it structured; what topics are coming up and how many questions are there? Then work systematically through it from the beginning, but keep an eye on the time. When you fall behind shorten your answers and leave difficult topics for the end.

Underline or highlight the important information/data in the question. If just names for compounds are given, write the chemical formula above it (e.g. sulfuric acid -> H_2SO_4).

Circle the functional groups in an organic formula and name them. Draw the carbons and hydrogens in skeletal formulae or displayed formulae if the structural formulae are given.

Make sure you read the question thoroughly and be aware what actions are expected from you from the command words used.

Identify the topic of the question and mentally bring up the flashcards associated to the topic. They will help you with the answer. If you have problems understanding the question, read it again slowly and also read through the follow up sub-questions (a, b, c etc.) sometimes the topic and the initial question becomes clearer. If you still do not understand the question or cannot come up with all the answers, do not spend any more time on it. Write down your best answers or just standard keywords/phrases from the flashcard. Writing something is better than writing nothing. You might still get some marks for it. Circle the question and come back to it at the end of the exam.

If you do calculations, write down a list of the data given (time permitting – otherwise just underline) and the formulae/equations which you are using (even if your calculation is wrong, you might get a mark for the correct formula).

Always show your workings and do the unit calculations. This means writing the units next to the numbers and cancelling or multiplying them accordingly. You should get the correct unit for your final answer. If not, you might not have converted them correctly (e.g. cm^3 into dm^3) or have used the wrong equation.

After writing down the final answer check if it makes sense (is the number in the expected range; does it have the correct sign in front, e. g. – for an exothermic reaction etc.).

Calculation answers should always be given in decimals, never fractions. Furthermore make sure you have answered all the questions and everything asked for (e.g. state symbols, significant figures etc.). Do not spend too much time on a question. Rule of thumb is 1 min per mark. If you are unsure, circle the question and come back to it at the end of the exam.

More tips about how to plan your revision and how to prepare for exams can be found on my website: https://www.alevelchemistryrevision.co.uk

Disclaimer: Due to the changing nature of mark schemes it cannot be guaranteed that answers according to these notes will give you full marks. These notes constitute only a part of a full revision program, alongside other methods like practising past papers. They have been created with great care; however, errors or omissions cannot be excluded.

Paper 1 (8462)
Topic 1 – Atomic Structure and the Periodic Table

Basic Definitions

Definition of atom

Atoms consist of…

Table of subatomic particles with mass and charge

Definition of Element

Definition of Isotopes

Atomic number

Mass number

Definition of Ion

Names of positive and negative ions

Definition of relative atomic mass with equation

Definition of relative formula mass

Definition of hazard

Definition of risk

Basic Definitions

Atom: smallest unit of an element
- consist of electrons organized in shells and a nucleus made from protons and neutrons (radius ~ 0.1 nanometres).
- nearly all of the mass of the atom is in the nucleus.
- radius of nucleus is 1/10,000 of the radius of the atom.

Subatomic Particle	Relative mass	Charge
Proton	1	+1
Neutron	1	0
Electron	very small	-1

Element: same kind of atoms (same atomic number).

Isotopes: atoms with same number of protons but different number of neutrons.
=> same element: same atomic number but different mass number.

Atomic number: number of protons.
-> equals number of electrons => charges cancel out.

Mass number: protons + neutrons

Ion: charged particle (different numbers of protons and electrons)
positive -> **cation** (more protons than electrons)
negative -> **anion** (more electrons than protons)
=> formed when an atom gains or loses electrons to get a full outer shell.

Relative Atomic mass A_r
Is the average mass of an element's isotopes [no unit].

$$A_r = \frac{(a\% \times A_1) + (b\% \times A_2)}{100}$$

a%: percentage of Isotope 1
b%: percentage of Isotope 2
A_1: Relative Isotopic mass of Isotope 1
A_2: Relative Isotopic mass of Isotope 2

Relative Formula Mass M_r
of a compound is the sum of the relative atomic masses of all its atoms [no unit].

Hazard: anything that could harm or damage.
Risk: probability of somebody being harmed.

Atomic Models & Electronic Structure

Four atomic models:
Dalton, Thomson, Rutherford, Bohr, (Chadwick)

Meaning of electronic structure

Six rules to determine electronic structure:

Electrons fill up...

Number of electrons per shell for the first three shells

Period number tells...

Atomic number tells....

Distribute...

(For cations and anions....)

Examples N and S with diagrams

Atomic Models

Dalton: solid spheres

Thomson: positively charged spheres with negative electrons embedded
-> 'plum pudding model'

Rutherford: small positive nucleus surrounded by a cloud of negative electrons
-> nuclear model (small number of alpha particles are deflected back)

Bohr: electrons orbit the nucleus in shells with fixed distances

Chadwick: discovered neutrons in nucleus (which also contains protons)

Electronic Structure

-> Distribution of electrons across the shells (energy levels)

Rules to determine the electronic structure
- Electrons fill up the lowest energy levels first
- Number of elements in the period indicates how many electrons are needed to fill the shell:
  1st shell   2
  2nd shell   8
  3rd shell   8
- Period number tells number of shells
- Atomic number tells total number of electrons
- Distribute the total number over the shells to get electron configuration
- *For cations take off electrons, for anions add electrons according to charge*

Examples
N: 2, 5 (total 7: 2 electrons in first shell, 5 in second/outer shell)

S: 2, 8, 6 (total 16: 2 electrons in first, 8 in second, 6 in last/outer shell)

Periodic Table

Arranged by...

Group number tells…

Period number tells…

Four group names

Mendeleev (two points)

Elements existing as diatomic molecules

Position and properties of metals (two points)

Position and properties of non-metals (two points)

Position and properties of transition metals (eight points)

Periodic Table

-> arranged by proton number

Group number
-> number of outer electrons => determines chemical properties & reactions
=> same group similar properties (periodic pattern)

Period number
-> number of shells

Group Names

Gr 1	**Alkali metals**
Gr 7	**Halogens**
Gr 0 (8)	**Noble Gases**
Gr III – XII	**Transition metals**

Mendeleev
- Early version of periodic table: Elements arranged by atomic mass (protons not yet discovered).
- Left gaps for undiscovered elements to have elements with similar chemical properties in same group. Made predictions about their properties, which were later confirmed, supporting his idea.

Elements existing as diatomic molecules (pairs of atoms)
$H_2, N_2, O_2,$ **Halogens:** F_2, Cl_2, Br_2, I_2 *(Have No Fear Of Ice-Cold Beer)*

Metals
- Left side of periodic table
- Form positive ions by losing electrons to gain full outer shell

Non-Metals
- Right side of periodic table (dividing line to metals between B and At)
- Share electrons or form negative ions by gaining electrons to gain full outer shell

Transition Metals
- Between Group 2 and 3
- Good conductors (Cu wires)
- Dense, strong, hard, shiny metals
- Less reactive than group 1 metals
- Higher melting points than group 1 metals
- They are good catalysts, e.g. Ni for hydrogenation or Fe for Haber
- They form coloured compounds
- They can have a variety of different charges as ions, e.g. Cu^+, Cu^{2+}

Group 1 Alkali Metals

Number of outer electrons

Properties

Reaction products (two points)

Reactions with:

Water

Oxygen

Chlorine

Dot-cross diagram of the reaction of Na with chlorine

Their oxides and hydroxides are...

Periodic trends down group:

Atomic radius

Reactivity (two points)

Atomic mass

Melting and boiling points

Group 1 – Alkali Metals

One electron in outer shell -> very reactive
=> similar properties: soft, low density.

Reactions of the Alkali Metals

-> easily loose electron to form ionic compounds
-> these are white solids that dissolve in water as colourless solutions

React vigorously with water to produce hydroxides and hydrogen gas
-> the hydrogen gas fizzes and burns -> explosive!
-> the water becomes alkaline (pH indicator changes colour) -> corrosive!
=> that's why they are called '**Alkali** Metals'

$2Na_{(s)} + 2H_2O_{(l)} \rightarrow 2NaOH_{(aq)} + H_{2(g)}$

They burn spontaneously with oxygen to produce white oxides (tarnish)
$4Na_{(s)} + O_{2(g)} \rightarrow 2Na_2O_{(s)}$ (+ N_2O_2 sodium peroxide)
Potassium produces a mixture of K_2O_2 (peroxide) and KO_2 (superoxide)

They react vigorously with Chlorine to produce white chlorine salts
$2Na_{(s)} + Cl_{2(g)} \rightarrow 2NaCl_{(s)}$

Simplified Dot-Cross diagrams of this reaction (outer shells only):

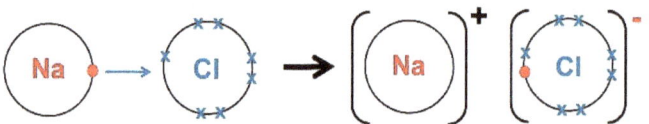

-> see revision card 'Redox Reactions'

Group 1 & 2 oxides, hydroxides are bases (neutralization)
-> see revision card 'Bases'

Periodic Trends down group

Atomic & Ionic Radius increases down group
-> more shells

Reactivity increases
-> electrons more easily lost (more shells, further from the nucleus)
=> more violent reaction; more energy given off

Atomic mass increases

Melting and boiling points decrease
-> see revision card 'Metallic Bonding'

Group 7 Halogens
&
Group 0 Noble Gases

Halogens exist as...
Number of outer electrons
Table with properties
Reactions:
With metals
With non-metals
Displacement reaction with equation (two points)
Periodic trends down group:
Reactivity
Atomic mass
Melting and boiling points

Number of outer electrons in noble gases
Reactivity of noble gases
Periodic trend of boiling point down group

Group 7 Halogens

Diatomic molecules (pairs of atoms)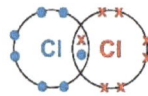

Seven electrons in outer shell => similar reactions

F_2	yellow gas	very toxic	
Cl_2	green gas	toxic	**reacts with H_2O**
Br_2	red-brown liquid	toxic	
I_2	grey solid / purple vapour		

Reactions

They form halide salts with metals -> ionic structures
  Metal + Halogen -> Halide Salts (redox)
  $2Na_{(s)}$ + $Cl_{2(g)}$ -> $2NaCl_{(s)}$

They form molecules with non-metals -> simple molecular structures
  $H_{2(g)}$ + $Cl_{2(g)}$ -> $2HCl_{(g)}$

Displacement Reaction
- to identify halide ions
- **more reactive** halogen displaces (oxidises) the ion of the **less reactive**
  -> higher up in group => higher oxidizing strength
  $Cl_{2(g)}$ + $2Br^-_{(aq)}$ -> $Br_{2(aq)}$ + $2Cl^-_{(aq)}$ Orange Solution
    0   *-1*   *0*   *-1*

Periodic Trends down group

- **Reactivity decreases**
  -> outer shell further away from the positive nucleus
  => less attraction for outer electrons
  => less likely to gain a negative electron
  => reaction less vigorous

- **Atomic mass increases**

- **Melting and boiling points increase**
  -> see revision card 'Intermolecular Forces'

Group 0 – Noble Gases

Full outer shell: eight electrons, except helium (2) -> do not react: **inert**
=> similar properties (monoatomic gases)

Periodic Trend down group

Boiling points increase
More electrons cause greater intermolecular forces
-> more energy needed to overcome these forces

Collecting Data

Accuracy

Repeatability

Random error

Systematic error

Zero error

Mean

Anomalous result

Significant figures

Rounding

How to find number of significant figures (two points)

Range

Reproducibility

Resolution

Precision

Definition of uncertainty with causes and equation

How to reduce uncertainty

Collecting Data

Accuracy: how close the result is to the true value (depends on method).

Repeatability: repeat a reading at least three times (results should be similar).

- The more times an experiment is repeated the more **precise** (close to the mean value) the results become.
- This reduces effect of **random errors** (e.g. limitation of accuracy of pipette: getting 49.9 ml or 50.1 ml when measuring 50 ml; human error).
- But the result can still be wrong due to a **systematic error**: e.g. balance was not zeroed -> always 0.5 g to heavy => **Zero Error.**
- Calculate the **mean** (average) of your results and ignore values which do not match: **anomalous results** -> try to find their reason.
- Write the answer with the appropriate number of **significant figures**: always use the lowest number of significant figures.
  e.g. if the data are given in 2 and 3 significant figures then the answer should be given in 2 significant figures. Write **(2 s.f.)** behind your answer.
- If the last non-significant figure of your final answer is 1 - 4 round down, if 5 – 9 round up. Do not round whilst still calculating.

Significant Figures:
- The first significant figure is the first digit which is not zero: 0.0109
- The other significant figures then follow (even if there is a zero): 0.0109
  -> In this example 0.0109 has three significant figures.

Range: how spread out the data are
-> Subtract the smallest number from the largest
Example: volumes of three titrations: 28.5, 27.9, 27.4 cm^3; range: **1.1 cm^3**

Reproducibility: do a second set of readings with another instrument.

Resolution: is the smallest change an instrument can detect, e.g. balance 0.1 g
-> a measuring instrument has to be sensitive enough (cannot weigh 0.4 g with a balance of 1 g resolution; need one with 0.1 g resolution).

Precision: depends on the sensitivity of the instrument, e.g. burette (precision: 0.1 cm^3) will be more precise than a beaker (precision: ~20 cm^3).

Uncertainty

Definition: The amount of error the measurement might have.
-> uncertainties are due to the limits in the resolution and random errors.

$$\text{Uncertainty} = \frac{\text{range}}{2}$$

Example above: +/- **0.55 cm^3**

To reduce uncertainty, increase value of reading, e.g. use larger volume or mass (or use equipment with higher resolution)

Separation Techniques

Six methods to separate mixtures:

Filtration (one point)

Evaporation (three points)

Crystallisation (four points)

Paper Chromatography:

Function

Eight points

Separation Techniques (Practical)

Physical Methods to separate mixtures of elements or compounds
- Filtration
- Evaporation
- Crystallisation
- Paper Chromatography
- Simple Distillation
- Fractional Distillation

Filtration
- Insoluble solid (product or impurity) is separated from liquid

Evaporation
- Soluble solid (salt) is separated from liquid by heating in evaporating dish
- Solvent evaporates -> solution gets more concentrated. Keep heating until dry crystals are formed and no liquid is left
- Quick, but cannot be used for compounds which decompose when heated

Crystallisation
- Heat solution gently in evaporating dish until crystals are formed (see above).
- But then stop heating with liquid still left in the dish
- When it cools down larger crystals form
- These are filtered out and dried in a drying oven or desiccator

Paper Chromatography
-> Separating components of a mixture, e.g. dyes in black ink
- Spot mixture (ink) on a pencil baseline on filter paper
- Put paper in a beaker filled with solvent (water, ethanol) below the baseline and cover beaker with a lid (prevents evaporation)
- Solvent travels up carrying different components (dyes) with it
- The plate is taken out when sufficient separation is achieved and solvent front reaches the top (end point)
- Different compounds travel at different rates to different places
- This is due to the different solubility in the solvent and the different attraction to the paper of the compounds
- The higher the solubility and the less attraction, the higher up the compound will travel (insoluble dyes will stay at the baseline)
- The resulting pattern of spots shows the number of different dyes => **Chromatogram**
- See also revision card 'Chromatography'

Simple Distillation
&
Fractional Distillation

Purpose of Distillation

Diagram

Description of simple distillation (eight points)

Description of fractional distillation (four points)

Simple and Fractional Distillation (Practical)

-> To separate different fractions of a mixture of liquids by their boiling points

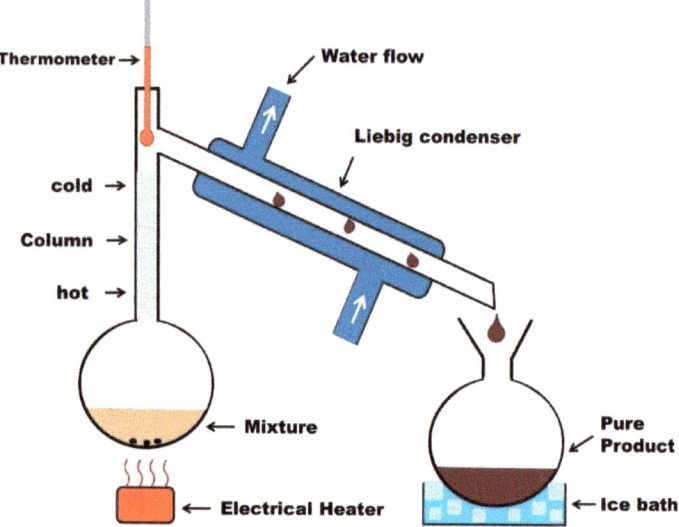

Simple Distillation
- Only separates compounds with very different boiling points
- See apparatus above, but with empty vertical glass column
- After a reaction: mixture of products and unreacted reactants present
- The desired product is separated from the mixture by heating
- Compounds with lower boiling points evaporate first
- They condense in the Liebig-condenser and are collected
- The cooled collection vessel is changed when the **boiling point** of the desired product is reached (indicated by the thermometer: the temperature remains constant for a while)
- This pure product is then collected and stored

Fractional Distillation
- Separates compounds with relative similar boiling points
- See apparatus as above: vertical glass column is filled with glass rods
- This Fractionating Column keeps the liquid with the higher boiling point condensing back into the reaction vessel because it is cooler at the top
- The liquid with the lower boiling point reaches the top of the column and the Liebig condenser
- The collection vessels are frequently changed for each separate fraction

Topic 2 – Bonding, Structure and Properties of Matter

Ionic and Covalent Compounds and Bonds

Definition of compound

Names and characteristics of ionic compounds (five points)

Three physical properties

Definition of ionic bond

Draw lattice

Names and characteristics of covalent compounds (five points)

Three physical properties

Definition of covalent bond

Intermolecular forces (three points)

Ionic and Covalent Compounds and Bonds

Compound: Atoms of different elements bonded together

Ionic compounds - Salts: Metal/Non-metal
- Consist of ions (charged particles)
- Ions are formed when an atom gains or loses electrons to get a full outer shell (more stable) -> see revision card 'Redox Reactions'
- 'Dot-and Cross' diagram: square bracket with charge around ion
- Form **giant ionic lattice** with alternating charges (see diagram below)
- Chemical formula gives ratio
- Physical properties:
    - high melting points: strong ionic bonds/forces, lots of energy needed.
    - soluble in water.
    - conduct electricity in solution or when molten: ions can move freely.
    - not conducting electricity when solid: ions (charges) cannot move.
- Examples: $NaCl$, $MgCl_2$

Ionic bond: electrostatic attraction between oppositely charged ions

$$Na^+ \; Cl^- \; Na^+ \; Cl^- \; Na^+ \; Cl^-$$
$$Cl^- \; Na^+ \; Cl^- \; Na^+ \; Cl^- \; Na^+$$
$$Na^+ \; Cl^- \; Na^+ \; Cl^- \; Na^+ \; Cl^-$$
$$Cl^- \; Na^+ \; Cl^- \; Na^+ \; Cl^- \; Na^+$$

Covalent compounds - Molecules: Non-metals
- Collection of atoms
- Atoms share electrons from the outer shell to get a full outer shell like noble gases (more stable) -> see covalent bond below
- 'Dot-and Cross' diagram: overlapping circles for bonds
- Form **simple molecular structures**
- Formula tells which atoms are directly connected to each other
- Physical properties:
    - low melting point: weak intermolecular forces, less energy needed.
    - not soluble in water.
    - not conducting electricity (no free electrons or ions).
- Examples: CH_4, H_2O, HCl, H_2, N_2 => simple molecular substances

Covalent bond: sharing a pair of electrons
-> strong electrostatic attraction between two nuclei (+) and the shared pair of electrons (-) => very strong and difficult to break

Intermolecular Forces of Simple Molecular Substances
- Responsible for **melting and boiling points** of **small molecules**
- The **more electrons** the stronger the force
- The **larger** the molecule the stronger the force -> higher melting point
    => more energy is required to overcome these forces of attraction

Giant Covalent Structures
&
Metallic Bonding

Definition of giant covalent structures
Melting point
Two elements which form giant covalent structures
Definition of allotropes
Four allotropes of carbon with properties
Silicon dioxide

Definition of metallic bonding
Melting points
(Trends of melting point across period)
Melting points of transition metals
Trends of melting point down group (two points)
Characteristics of metals (three points)
Diagram of structure

Giant Covalent Structures

- **Definition**: Network of covalently bonded atoms (**Macromolecules**).
- High melting points: Large energy needed to break strong covalent bonds.
- C, Si => four covalent bonds (Group 4).

Allotropes: Different structural forms of the same element (same physical state)

Allotropes of carbon
    Diamond: 4 bonds —> hard, high melting point,
              not conducting electricity, *insoluble*
    Graphite: 3 bonds, sheets of hexagons held together weakly -> slippery, soft
            (lubricating), high melting point, single electrons are **delocalized**
            and **conduct electricity**
    Graphene: one layer (sheet) of carbon atoms (graphite) -> **two-dimensional**
            Strong, light & thin -> added to composite materials for strength
            => structure and characteristics like graphite
    Fullerene: 3 bonds, pentagons, hexagons (like graphite), heptagons
            -> spheres and nanotubes

Silicon dioxide: hard, high melting point, not conducting electricity
                => **sand (silica, SiO_2)**, *quartz*

Metallic Bonding

Definition: Electrostatic attraction between metal **cations (+)** and **delocalized electrons (-)** from the outer shell.
-> high melting points: large energy required to overcome strong attraction.

Across the period higher melting points:
- more delocalized electrons & charges of cations increase: Na^+, Mg^{2+}
- -> transition metals have higher melting points than group 1 & 2 metals

Down the group lower melting points:
- more shells
- greater distance

Characteristics of metals:
- electrical & thermal conductors: transferred by free moving electrons
- malleable: layers can slide
- soft –> only alloys are hard: different sized atoms distort the layers

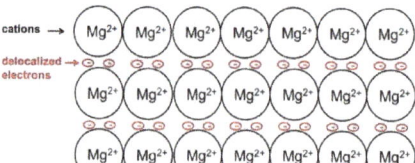

Giant metallic lattice

States of Matter

Physical state depends on…

The stronger the force…

Strength of attractions depends on… (three points)

Three states according to particle theory:

Solid (three points)

Word for solid becoming a liquid

Word for liquid becoming a solid

Liquid (three points)

Two words for liquid becoming a gas

Word for gas becoming a liquid

Gas (two points)

Predicting the state at room temperature (three points)

Four state symbols

States of Matter

Physical state of matter depends on the forces of attraction between its particles -> the stronger the forces, the more energy is needed to overcome them to change states

Strength of attractions depends on
- Material (structure, type of bond)
- Temperature
- Pressure

Three states - particle theory (particle -> small, solid, inelastic sphere)

I) Solid
- Strong forces keep particles in fixed positions -> keep shape & volume
- Heating lets particles vibrate -> slight expansion of lattice
- Further heating weakens forces between particles until they break free:
  => **Melting** into a liquid

Freezing: liquid is cooled down until bonds form to become a solid

II) Liquid
- Weak forces enable particles to move freely, but still stick together
  -> definite volume but no definite shape: will fill container from bottom
- Heating increases random movement -> slight expansion of liquid
- Further heating weakens forces between particles until they break free:
  => **Boiling (Evaporating)** into a gas

Condensation: gas is cooled down until bonds form to become a liquid

III) Gas
- Very weak forces enable particles to move freely away from each other
  -> no definite volume or shape: will fill container completely
- Heating increases random motion -> great expansion, increased pressure

Predicting the state of a substance at Room Temperature (RT = 25 °C)
- Melting point above room temperature   => Solid
- Melting point below room temperature   => Liquid
- Boiling point below room temperature   => Gas
-> same patterns for any other temperature

State Symbols

s = solid, l = liquid, g = gas, **aq** = aqueous (solution in water)

Nanoparticles

Definition

Properties and applications (five points)

Fullerene

Properties, shapes and applications (five points)

Nanoparticles

Definition: Small particles of a size between 1 – 100 nm *(1nm = 10^{-9} m)*

Properties and applications
- Large surface area to volume ratio (ratio = surface area / volume) -> good catalysts
- The smaller the particle the larger this ratio
- Nanomedicine: easily absorbed by the body (fullerenes)
- Silver nanoparticles -> kill bacteria (wound dressing)
- Cosmetics: sunscreen & moisturisers
- Health and environmental risks have still to be investigated (might damage human cells or environment)

Fullerenes
- Large Carbon molecules (60 – 100 C atoms) -> Allotrope of carbon
- One carbon has three bonds and one free electron which can conduct electricity and heat
- Arranged as pentagons, hexagons (like graphite), or heptagons
- Shaped like hallow **balls** (**Buckminster Fullerene C_{60}**)
  -> can be used to deliver drugs (cage), as catalyst or as lubricant
- Or shaped like closed **tubes** (**nanotubes**) -> very strong and light
  => to strengthen graphite (tennis racket) or in electronics

Fine Particles: 100 nm – 2,500 nm

Coarse Particles: 2,500 nm – 10,000 nm

Topic 3 – Quantitative Chemistry

Mole
&
Molar Gas Volume

Definition of mole

Equation to calculate mole from mass

Equation to calculate number of particles from moles

Molar gas volume at standard conditions

Equation for calculating volume of gas from moles

Converting cm^3 into dm^3

Volumes are proportional to....

The ratios of the volumes of reactants and products....

Mole

Def.: 1 mole = *6.02 x 10²³* **particles** (atoms, molecules, ions, electrons etc.)
-> **Avogadro's number** N_A, *(given)*

$$n = \frac{m}{M_r}$$

n: number of moles [mol]
m: mass [g]
M_r: relative formula mass [g/mol]
[ ]: units

$$N = n \times N_A$$

N: number of particles [no unit]
N_A: Avogadro's number 6.02 x 10²³ [mol⁻¹]

Standard form: $0.001 = 1 \times 10^{-3}$ -> can be used in calculations

Molar Gas Volume

Volume of **1 mole** of any **gas** = *24 dm³ (given)*
-> at **standard conditions** **(RT 25° C, 100 kPa)**

$$V_x = n \times 24 \text{ dm}^3 \text{ mol}^{-1}$$

V_x: unknown volume [dm³]
n: number of moles [mol]

Converting cm³ into dm³:

$$x \text{ cm}^3 = \frac{x}{1000} \text{ dm}^3$$

Volumes are proportional to moles

-> the ratios of the volumes of reactants and products can be used to work out the mole equation (reaction equation) and vice versa:

Example

How much carbon monoxide is produced when an excess of carbon reacts with 40 cm³ of oxygen?

$$2C_{(s)} + O_{2(g)} \rightarrow 2CO_{(g)}$$

1 mole O_2 forms 2 moles CO, hence 40 cm³ O_2 form 80 cm³ CO

Calculate Masses from Mole Equation
&
Work out Reaction Equation from Masses

Tip

Five calculation steps

Rule for rounding

How to write answer

Limiting reactant

Three calculation steps to work out reaction equation from masses

Example calculation

Calculate Masses from Mole Equations

-> if the mass of one substance and the mole equation are given, then the mass of another substance of this reaction can be worked out:

a) Underline or highlight all data given in the exam question.
1) Calculate moles for the given compound by using $n = m / M_r$
2) **Highlight** mole numbers of related compounds (given and unknown)
3) Get mole factor by dividing mole number of unknown compound (3) by the mole number of given compound (4)
4) Multiply moles of given compound with factor to get moles of unknown
5) Calculate mass of unknown compound by using $m = n \times M_r$
- Do not round whilst still calculating
- Write the answer with the appropriate number of significant figures
- If the masses of two reactants are given, calculate the moles and use the **smaller value** (take mole ratios into account) to calculate moles of product -> **limiting reactant**

Example
a) Calculate amount of O_2 (in grams) produced if 3.24 g of $Fe(NO_3)_3$ is heated

$$4Fe(NO_3)_3 \rightarrow 2Fe_2O_3 + 12NO_2 + 3O_2$$

1) Moles $Fe(NO_3)_3$: n = 3.24 g/ 241.8 g/mol = 0.0134 moles
2) See **mole equation** above: 4 & 3
3) Factor for O_2: 3/4 = 0.75
4) Moles O_2: 0.75 x 0.0134 moles = 0.01005 moles
5) Mass O_2: m = n x M = 0.01005 mol x 32 g/mol = 0.322 g (3 s.f.)

Work out Reaction Equation from Masses

-> if the masses of all substances (reactants and products) of a chemical reaction are given, the mole (symbol) equation of this reaction can be worked out:

- Use $n=m/M_r$ to calculate moles of each substance
- Divide by smallest mole number to get mole ratios of mole equation
- If one of these is not a whole number, multiply all by the same amount so that all become whole numbers

Example calculation
48 g of **carbon** burn with **64 g** of **oxygen** to produce **112 g** of **carbon monoxide**. What is the balanced symbol equation for this reaction?

M_r (C) = 12 M_r (O_2) = 2 x 16 = 32 M_r (CO) = 12 + 16 = 28

C: $\underline{48}$ = 4 moles O_2: $\underline{64}$ = 2 moles   CO: $\underline{112}$ = 4 moles
    12   32   28

C: 4/2 = 2 O_2: 2/2 = 1   CO: 4/2 = 2   -> ratios

Answer: $2C_{(s)}$ + $O_{2(g)}$ -> $2CO_{(g)}$

Percentage Mass & Percentage Yield

Equation to calculate percentage mass
Example calculation

Equation to calculate percentage yield
Physical quantities of yield
Three reasons for loss
Example calculation

Percentage Mass of an Element in a Compound

$$\text{\%-mass} = \frac{n \times A_r}{M_r} \times 100$$

A_r: relative atomic mass of the element
M_r: relative formula mass of the compound
n: moles of the element in chemical formula (subscripted number)

Example calculation

What is percentage mass (percentage composition) of Cl in $MgCl_2$?

$$\text{\%-mass} = \frac{2 \times 35.5}{(24 + 2 \times 35.5)} \times 100$$

%-mass = 75%

Percentage Yield

$$\text{percentage yield} = \frac{\text{actual yield}}{\text{theoretical yield}} \times 100$$

Physical quantities of actual and theoretical yield of products can be mass [grams] or moles [moles]

-> In industry high yield are desired to reduce waste and costs

Reasons for loss
- Reaction not complete (reversible reaction)
- Loss of product (sticking to vessel, evaporation of liquids)
- By-products

Example calculation

A chemist made $MgCl_2$ by reacting Mg with chlorine gas. He calculated a theoretical yield of 20 g. His actual yield was 18 g. What is the percentage yield?

$$\text{percentage yield} = \frac{18 \text{ g}}{20 \text{ g}} \times 100 = 90\%$$

Atom Economy & Concentrations

Equation for atom economy

Three rules

Benefits of high atom economy (four points)

Example calculation

Equation for mole concentration

Converting dm^3 in cm^3

Equation for mass concentration

Converting mole concentration into mass concentration

Atom Economy

$$\% \text{ atom economy} = \frac{M_r \text{ desired product}}{\Sigma M_r \text{ all products}} \times 100$$

Σ: sum

- The higher the percentage the 'greener' the process
- 100 % for addition reactions (only one product)
- Multiply M_r with mole numbers from chemical equations

Environmental and economic benefits of high atom economy
- Avoiding waste (products which are of no use)
- High sustainability (less raw material)
- More profitable (raw material and removal of waste products expensive)
- High efficiency

Example calculation

$(NH_4)_2SO_{4(s)} + 2NaOH_{(aq)} \rightarrow 2NH_{3(g)} + Na_2SO_{4(aq)} + 2H_2O_{(l)}$

Calculate the percentage atom economy for the production of ammonia

$$\% \text{ atom economy} = \frac{2 \times 17}{2 \times 17 + 142 + 2 \times 18} \times 100$$

$$= 16.0\%$$

Concentration

Mole concentration:

$$c = \frac{n}{V}$$

n: moles [mol]
V: volume [dm^3]
c: concentration [mol dm^{-3}]

1 dm^3 = 1000 cm^3

Mass concentration:

$$c_m = \frac{m}{V}$$

m: mass [g]
c: mass concentration [g dm^{-3}]

Convert mole concentration into mass concentration:

$$c_m = M_r \times c$$

Topic 4 – Chemical Changes

Acids and Bases

Definition of acid
Four important acids
Difference between strong and weak acids
Reaction of acids with bases with type of reaction
Reaction of acids with metals with type of reaction

Definition of base
Three bases with reaction equations
Definition of Alkali
Two tests for acids and bases

Acids

Definition: An acid is a substance with a pH of less than 7. It forms H^+ ions (protons) in water (ionise).

Important acids:
HCl   hydrochloric acid (hydrogen chloride) – s
H_2SO_4 sulphuric acid - s
HNO_3 nitric acid - s
CH_3COOH ethanoic acid - w

Strong acids (s):
Completely dissociated in H_2O: HCl   -> H^+ + Cl^-
Strong acid can be diluted with water -> less concentrated (less acidic)

Weak acids (w):
Partially dissociated: CH_3COOH ⇌ CH_3COO^- + H^+
=> equilibrium: less H^+ ions -> less reactive => slower reactions
=> higher pH than strong acids with same concentration

Acids react with bases to form salts and water
    HCl + NaOH -> NaCl + H_2O
-> Acid-base reaction: **Neutralisation** (product water is neutral)

Acids reacting with metals forming salts and hydrogen
    Mg + H_2SO_4 -> $MgSO_4$ + H_2
-> Redox reaction

Bases

Definition: A base is a substance with a pH of greater than 7. It forms OH^- ions in water.

Metal oxides *(s)* **(Acid-Base Reaction)**
    MgO + 2HCl -> $MgCl_2$ + H_2O

Hydroxides *(s)*
    $Ca(OH)_2$ + 2HCl -> $CaCl_2$ + $2H_2O$ Neutralises acid soils

Carbonates *(w)*
    $CaCO_3$ + 2HCl -> $CaCl_2$ + H_2O + CO_2 Fizzing, $CaCO_3$ disappears
    => acid test

An **Alkali** is a soluble base: base that dissolves in water and releases OH^-

Tests for acids and bases
- pH indicator changes colour, e.g. litmus red (acid) -> blue (base)
- pH meter shows value lower (acid) or greater (base) than 7

pH
&
Titrations

pH scale

pH expresses....

The lower the pH the...

Change by 1 pH unit...

How to measure pH

Purpose of titration

Function of Indicator

Three indicators with their colour changes

Endpoint

Titration steps

Accuracy of volume measurement

pH

pH scale: **0** acidic < **7** neutral < alkaline **14**

- pH expresses the H^+ concentration in the solution *(pH = -log[H$^+$])*.
- the lower the pH the higher the H^+ concentration and the more acidic.
- change by **1 pH unit**, changes the **H^+ concentration** by the **factor 10**.
- pH can be measured with **pH meter** (electronically) or **universal indicator** (mixture of dyes, which shows gradual colour change).

Titrations (Practical)

-> method to determine a concentration.

Indicators
-> indicate pH jump by colour change at endpoint

phenolphthalein:	colourless (a)	-> pink (b)
methyl orange:	red (a)	-> yellow (b)
litmus:	red (a)	-> blue (b)
not universal indicator	-> too gradual colour change	

Endpoint: same number of moles of H^+ & OH^-.
 -> *pH of indicator colour change must match endpoint.*

Titration Steps for an Acid-Base Titration (Neutralisation)
- *flush burette with distilled H_2O and standard solution (water dilutes standard).*
- use a funnel to fill burette with standard solution above 0 and drain to 0 mark. (removes air bubbles in tap) -> wear safety glasses and keep eyes above funnel
- fill exact volume of unknown solution, with volumetric pipette, in conical flask
- add few drops of indicator (too much indicator would change pH).
- use white tile as background (to better see the colour change).
- do rough titration to get an idea for the endpoint: add solution & swirl until colour change.
- do accurate titration with dropwise addition of solution towards the end.
- repeat at least three times to get consistent results -> increases accuracy.
- record volumes of standard solution used (eyes level, bottom of meniscus).
- calculate the average volume (ignore values which do not match: > 0.1 cm^3).
- calculate moles of standard solution from this volume using n = c V.
- take mole ratios from reaction equation into account.
- calculate concentration of unknown solution by using c = n/V.

Accuracy of volume measurement
Pipette (fixed volume) > burette (variable volume) > measuring cylinder

List of Anions
&
Naming Salts
&
Making Soluble Salts from Insoluble Bases

Seven important anions

Rule for writing salt name and formula

Two rules for naming anions

Four steps for making soluble salts

Important Anions

chloride	Cl^-
carbonate	CO_3^{2-}
hydroxide	OH^-
sulphate	SO_4^{2-}
sulphide	S^{2-}
nitrate	NO_3^-
ethanoate	CH_3COO^-

Naming salts

First **cation (metal, +)** then **anion (non-metal, -)**: e.g. **NaCl** -> **sodium chloride**

Anion (negative ion)
Name of anion finishes with:

- **ide**   if anion consists of just one element like S^{2-},
             e.g. Ca**S** – calcium sulph**ide** or NaCl – sodium chlor**ide**

- **ate**   if anion consists of more than one element like SO_4^{2-} (sulphur & oxygen), e.g. Na₂**SO₄** – Sodium sulph**ate**

Making Soluble Salts from Insoluble Bases (Practical)

1) Neutralise warm acid with an excess of **insoluble metal carbonate**/hydroxide/oxide. Stir the mixture.

   $CaCO_{3(s)} + 2HCl_{(aq)} \rightarrow CaCl_{2(aq)} + H_2O_{(l)} + CO_{2(g)}$

2) Filter out the excess of **insoluble carbonate**/hydroxide/oxide (**CaCO₃**)

3) Evaporate the water of the remaining salt solution by gentle heating (water bath) until salt crystals (CaCl₂) are formed.
   Let the solution cool -> **Crystallisation**

4) The salt crystals are filtered out and dried

Note: sodium carbonate is a soluble base.

Redox Reactions
&
Displacement Reaction

Definition of oxidation

Definition of reduction

Redox

Five rules for redox reactions

Five common charges

Displacement reaction (two points)

Examples

Redox Reactions

Oxidation **I**s **L**oss of electrons (gain of oxygen)
-> when atoms (metals) lose electrons then positive ions (cations) are formed

Reduction **I**s **G**ain of electrons (loss of oxygen)
-> when atoms (non-metals) gain electrons, negative ions (anions) are formed

=> **OILRIG**

REDuction and **OX**idation occur together -> **REDOX**

Rules:
- group number indicates how many electrons are lost or gained to get a full outer shell:
- Group 1 and 2 like to lose 1 or 2 electrons respectively
- Group 6 and 7 like to gain 2 or 1 electrons respectively
  -> e.g. for oxygen it is easier to gain 2 electrons than to lose 6
- A salt is neutral. Hence the charges of their ions have to be balanced by subscript numbers to add up to zero to get its chemical formula:
  Al_2O_3 $(2 \times +3) + (3 \times -2) = 0$
  $_{+3}$ $_{-2}$

  -> a lower-case number multiplies only the element in front of it
- Elements on their own do not have a charge: 0
- most common charges *(oxidation numbers)* of elements in compounds:
  Halogens (Gr. 7)   -1
  Oxygen, *Sulphur*   -2
  Hydrogen   +1
  Alkali metals (Gr. 1)   +1
  Alkaline earth metals (Gr.2)   +2

Displacement Reaction

- special case of redox reactions
- more reactive element (metal) displaces less reactive

Examples

$Zn_{(s)}$ + $FeSO_{4(aq)}$ -> $ZnSO_{4(aq)}$ + $Fe_{(s)}$
$_0$ $_{+2}$ $_{+2}$ $_0$

zinc + iron sulphate -> zinc sulphate + iron

$Cl_{2(g)}$ + $2KI_{(aq)}$ -> $I_{2(aq)}$ + $2KCl_{(aq)}$ **Brown Solution**
$_0$ $_{-1}$ $_0$ $_{-1}$

=> see also revision cards 'Metals and their Reactivity' and 'Group 7 Halogens'

Balancing Redox Equations
&
Conservation of Mass

Balancing a simple redox reaction (two points)

How to attain half equations
Important rule for redox reactions
Combine half equations to…
Example

Conservation of mass (four points)

Balancing Redox Equations

How to balance a simple redox equation (symbol equation)
- First write the **chemical formula of the product** to the right side of the arrow. Balance this formula with **subscript numbers** according to the **charges of the ions (group number)** by using lowest common multiple.
- Then balance whole equation by putting **numbers in front** of reactants and products (never change subscript numbers, as this would create a different substance).

$$4Al + 3O_2 \rightarrow 2Al_2O_3$$
$$_{0} _{0} _{+3\ -2} \quad \text{(lowest common multiple: 6)}$$

-> a **number in front** multiplies everything behind

Half-Equations
- split up redox reaction into two separate oxidation and reduction reactions => **half equations**
- **number of electrons transferred must be the same in overall equation**
  -> multiply to get lowest common multiple (here: 6)
- Combine half equations to an overall (ionic) equation

Example

Half equations:
Reduction: $Fe^{3+} + 3e^- \rightarrow Fe$ | x 2
Oxidation: $Zn \rightarrow Zn^{2+} + 2e^-$ | x 3

Overall $3Zn + 2Fe^{3+} \rightarrow 2Fe + 3Zn^{2+}$
$_{0} _{+3} _{0} _{+2}$

- For better explanations about redox reactions including oxidation states see revision cards in A-Level Flash Notes

Conservation of Mass

- During a chemical reaction, atoms are neither destroyed or created
- Hence on each side of the reaction there must be the same number of atoms
- Therefore, also no mass is lost or gained -> **mass is conserved:**
- The sum of the M_r of the reactants equals the sum of the M_r of the products

Metals and their Reactivity
&
Extraction of Metals from Ores

The Reactivity series

The more reactive the metal....

The higher up the more....

Reaction of metal with acid

Reaction of metal with water

Correlation between reactivity and speed

Methods to measure speed and reactivity

Correlation between reactivity and temperature change

Displacement reaction

Ores

How to get pure metals

Metals below carbon...

Metals above carbon...

Unreactive metals

Metals and their Reactivity

The Reactivity Series
Potassium   K
Sodium   Na
Calcium   Ca
Magnesium   Mg
Aluminium   Al
<u>Carbon   C</u>
Zinc   Zn
Iron   Fe
Hydrogen H_2
Copper   Cu

- **The more reactive the metal (higher up) the more easily it loses electrons (gets oxidised)**

- The higher up the more easily it reacts with acid or water *(above Mg)*.
  Metal + Acid -> Salt + Hydrogen   -> **word equation**
  $Mg_{(s)}$ + $2HCl_{(aq)}$ -> $MgCl_{2(aq)}$ + $H_{2(g)}$ -> **symbol equation**

  Metal + Water -> Metal Hydroxide + Hydrogen
  $Mg_{(s)}$ + $2H_2O_{(l)}$ -> $Mg(OH)_{2(aq)}$ + $H_{2(g)}$

- The more reactive the metal the faster it reacts (vigorously)
  => speed can be measured by the rate of which H_2 is produced

- The more reactive the metal the greater the temperature change of the reaction (exothermic)

- More reactive metal displaces less reactive metal -> **Displacement**
  See revision card 'Displacement Reaction'

Extraction of Metals from Ores

Ores: minerals containing enough metal for extraction
-> mostly oxides (oxidised by air: $2Mg + O_2$ -> **$2MgO$**)

Ores are **reduced** to get pure metal (oxygen is removed):

Metals below carbon are less reactive and can be extracted by reduction with carbon -> cheap, e.g. iron in blast furnace: $2Fe_2O_3 + 3C$ -> $4Fe + 3CO_2$

Metals above carbon are more reactive and have to be extracted using electrolysis -> expensive

Some **metals** are so **unreactive** that they are found as elements not oxides in the earth and do not need to be reduced: **gold, silver, platinum**

Electrolysis
&
Alternative Copper Extractions

Definition of electrolysis

Movements of anions and cations

Definition of electrode

Definition of electrolyte

The more reactive the metal....

Rules for positive electrode

Rules for negative electrode

Rule for molten salts

Reason for copper electrolysis

Reactions at anode and cathode of copper electrolysis

Electrolyte of copper electrolysis

Two alternative copper extraction methods

Electrolysis

- Passing electrical current through ionic substances (molten or in solution) breaks them down into the elements -> **Electrolysis**
- Negative ions (anions) move to **positive** electrode: **anode** -> **oxidation**
- Positive ions (cations) move to **negative** electrode: **cathode** -> **reduction**
- **Electrode:** a solid that conducts electricity and is submerged in electrolyte.
- **Electrolyte:** molten or dissolved (aqueous) ionic compound that conducts electricity. Ions are free to move to electrode. Insoluble salts need to be melted.

Rules

- **The more reactive the metal (higher up) the more easily it loses electrons (gets oxidised) and the more difficult to reduce it in electrolysis**

- **Positive electrode (anode):** Oxygen is produced, if the anion of the aqueous electrolyte is not a halide (F⁻, Cl⁻, Br⁻, I⁻). If it is a halide, then the halogen is produced.

- **Negative electrode (cathode):** Hydrogen is produced in an aqueous electrolyte, if the metal is more reactive (higher up in reactivity series) than hydrogen. The metal is produced, if it is less reactive than hydrogen.

- **Molten salts always form their elements:** e.g. $PbCl_2$ forms lead and chlorine.

   Anode (+): $2Cl^- \rightarrow Cl_2 + 2e^-$ (oxidation)
   Cathode (-): $Pb^{2+} + 2e^- \rightarrow Pb$ (reduction)

Copper Electrolysis

Copper ores can be reduced to copper by carbon but the product is too impure. Electrolysis is used instead to get pure **copper:**

Oxygen produced at **Anode** (no halides) (+): $4OH^-_{(aq)} \rightarrow O_{2(g)} + 2H_2O_{(l)} + 4e^-$
Pure copper is deposited at copper **Cathode** (-): $Cu^{2+}_{(aq)} + 2e^- \rightarrow Cu_{(s)}$

Electrolyte: aqueous $CuSO_4$ solution, containing also H^+ and OH^- ions.

Alternative Copper Extractions (Topic 10)

-> traditional copper mining is damaging to the environment.
-> alternatives for extracting copper from low-grade ores have been developed:

Bioleaching: bacteria extract copper ions from ores into solution **(leachate)** for electrolysis or displacement reaction (with scrap iron).

Phytomining: plants enrich copper from the soil in their leaves, which are burned. The ashes are subjected to electrolysis or displacement.

Aluminium Electrolysis
&
Sodium Chloride Electrolysis

Aluminium electrolysis (two points)

Reactions at anode and cathode

Overall reaction

Disadvantages of aluminium electrolysis (two points)

Raw material for sodium chloride electrolysis

Material for electrodes

Explanation of the cathode reaction

Reaction at anode

Reaction at cathode

Diagram of the electrolysis apparatus

Aluminium Electrolysis

- Aluminium is too reactive to get reduced by carbon
- Its melting point is too high: **Al_2O_3 (bauxite)** is molten together with **cryolite** *(Na_3AlF_6)* which lowers melting point

Anode + (carbon/graphite): $2O^{2-} \rightarrow O_2 + 4e^-$ | x 3
Cathode − (carbon lining): $Al^{3+} + 3e^- \rightarrow Al$ | x 4
Overall: $2Al_2O_3 \rightarrow 4Al + 3O_2$

Disadvantages:
-> High usage of electricity makes it **expensive** *(hydroelectric power station)*
-> Graphite anode needs regular replacement because $C + O_2 \rightarrow CO_2$

Sodium Chloride Electrolysis

- Raw material: concentrated brine (NaCl-solution)
- Graphite electrodes
- $Na^+ + e^- \rightarrow Na$ is expected, but sodium is more reactive than hydrogen, hence it is more difficult to reduce than hydrogen (H^+)
  -> H^+ gets reduced instead of Na^+ at cathode
  -> see revision cards 'Metals and their Reactivity' and 'Electrolysis'

Half equations
Anode (+): $2Cl^- \rightarrow Cl_2 + 2e^-$ (oxidation)
Cathode (−): $2H^+ + 2e^- \rightarrow H_2$ (reduction)

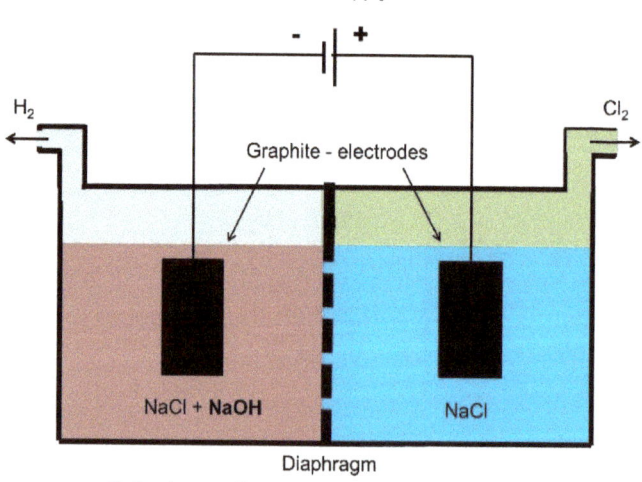

Two Main Types of Inorganic Reactions & Ionic Equations

Two main types

Two minor types

Ionic equations only show...

Definition of spectator ion

Example

Two Main Types of Inorganic Reactions

1) Redox (Reduction/Oxidation)
-> transfer of electrons *(charges change)*

$$4Al + 3O_2 \rightarrow 2Al_2O_3$$
$$0 0 {+3}\ {-2}$$

-> **Displacement** is a special case of redox reactions

2) Acid-Base (Neutralisation)
-> *transfer of protons* H^+ *(charges do not change)*

$$HCl + NaOH \rightarrow NaCl + H_2O$$
$$+1\ -1 \quad +1\ -2\ +1 \quad +1\ -1 \quad +1\ -2$$

Minor reaction types

- **Thermal decomposition**
  $$CaCO_{3(s)} \rightarrow CaO_{(s)} + CO_{2(g)}$$
  Limestone   Quicklime

- **Precipitation**
  $$Ag^+_{(aq)} + Cl^-_{(aq)} \rightarrow AgCl_{(s)}$$

-> No change of charges *(oxidation numbers)*

Ionic Equations

-> only show the reacting particles

Spectator Ions: Ions which do not take part in the reaction
They can be removed from the full equation to give an ionic equation

Example

Full equation:
$$Cl_2 + 2NaBr \rightarrow Br_2 + 2NaCl$$
$$0 \quad +1\ -1 \quad 0 \quad +1\ -1$$

Na^+ does not change oxidation states -> *spectator ion*, remove from equation:

Ionic equation:
$$Cl_2 + 2Br^- \rightarrow Br_2 + 2Cl^- \quad \text{Orange Solution}$$
$$0 \quad\ \ -1 \quad\ \ 0 \quad\ \ -1$$
Pale green

Topic 5 – Energy Changes

Electrochemical Cells
&
Cell Types

Definition of electrochemical cell

Where the voltage comes from (three points)

Battery (two points)

Diagram of a Cu/Zn Cell

Two types of batteries with properties

Description and advantages of fuel cells

Electrode reactions for hydrogen-oxygen fuel cell

Overall equation

Electrochemical Cells

Definition: Two different (metal) electrodes in an electrolyte (salt solution)
- The two different metals have different reactivities which result in a charge difference -> **voltage** (electricity), which is measured by a voltmeter
- The bigger the difference in reactivity the bigger the voltage -> see reactivity series => voltage can be predicted from other cells
- Different electrolytes can also change the voltage, because they react with the metal electrodes
- Several cells can be connected in series to create a higher voltage => **battery**
- Electrochemical cells are used in batteries to power electrical equipment

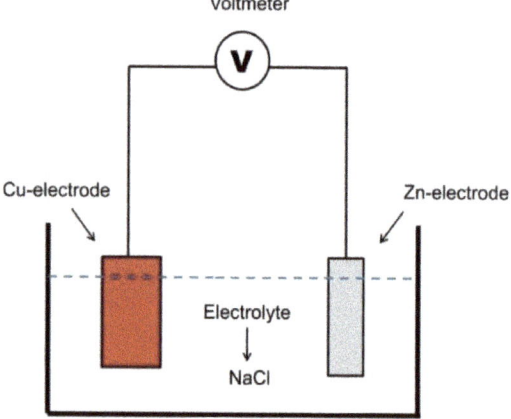

Cell Types

- **Non-rechargeable Batteries -> irreversible reactions**
  Reactants are used up, e.g. alkaline batteries (Zn/C).
  -> cheap, last longer but create more waste

- **Rechargeable Batteries -> reversible reactions**
  Can be recharged by external power supply.
  e.g. Lithium- or Ni/Cd batteries: used in laptops or mobile phones
  -> more power, saves money over time, but more toxic and expensive

- **Fuel Cells:** creates a voltage by reacting a fuel (H_2) with oxygen -> H_2O
  The fuel is fed into the cell.
  -> no recharging, no toxic waste (H_2O), no direct CO_2 emission, *but H_2 is explosive, difficult to store and needs energy to produce (fossil fuels)*

  Hydrogen-Oxygen Full Cell *(acidic)*
  Negative electrode Ox (-): $H_2 \rightarrow 2H^+ + 2e^-$ |x2
  Positive electrode Red (+): $4H^+ + O_2 + 4e^- \rightarrow 2H_2O$
  Overall: $2H_2 + O_2 \rightarrow 2H_2O$

Exothermic and Endothermic Reactions
&
Bond Energies
&
Calorimeter

Definitions for exothermic/endothermic with examples

Equation to calculate energy change from bond energies
Rule between mole equation and bond energies
Two rules regarding bond forming and breaking
Exothermic/endothermic in relation to bond energies

How to measure energy change of reaction
Experimental applications of these measurements
School apparatus to measure energy changes
(Diagram)

Exothermic and Endothermic Reactions

Exothermic   energy released into surroundings
　　　　　　　　-> rise in temperature (heat up)
　　　　　　　　e.g. Burning/Combustion (oxidation), Neutralization

Endothermic   energy taken from surroundings
　　　　　　　　-> fall in temperature (cool down)
　　　　　　　　e.g. thermal decomposition of $CaCO_3$; sports injury packs

Bond Energies

Bond energies H can be used to calculate the energy change of a reaction:

$\Delta H_r = \Sigma H$ **bonds broken** $- \Sigma H$ **bonds formed**

ΔH_r: Energy change of the reaction

==Multiply bond energies with mole numbers from reaction equation==

- Bond forming releases energy
- Bond breaking requires energy

If ΣH bonds formed $>$ ΣH bonds broken $\Rightarrow$ **exothermic**

If ΣH bonds formed $<$ ΣH bonds broken $\Rightarrow$ **endothermic**

Calorimeter (Practical)

- The energy change of a reaction can be determined by measuring the temperature of the solution before and after the reaction.

- Variables like mass or concentration can be changed to determine their effect on the energy change

- At school a **polystyrene cup** might be used as reaction vessel.
  To avoid head loss the cup needs an effective **insulation**:
  -> thick polystyrene walls and a lid

  Below is the diagram of a more sophisticated calorimeter:

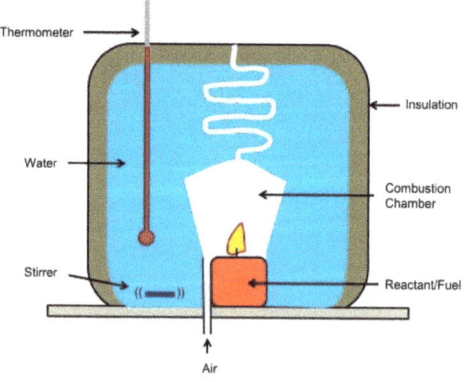

Reaction Profiles

Purpose

Definition activation energy

Energy level diagram of exothermic reaction

Reason why exothermic reaction releases energy

Energy level diagram of endothermic reaction

Tip

Reaction Profiles

-> show the energy changes of the reactants and products over the course of a reaction

Activation energy E_a: minimum amount of energy needed for reactants to collide *(braking bonds)* and start a chemical reaction -> always positive

Energy Level Diagrams (Reaction Profiles)

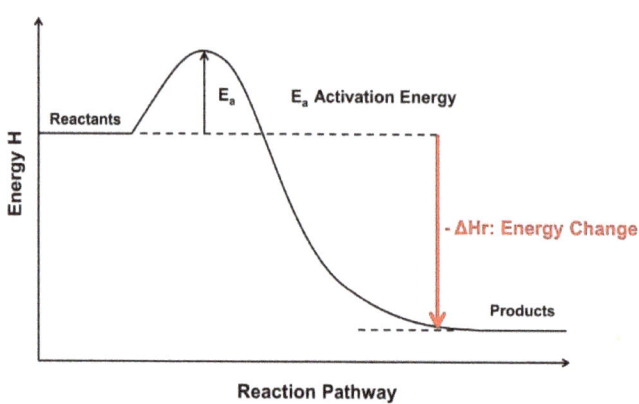

-> Energy $(-\Delta H_r)$ is released because products store less energy than reactants

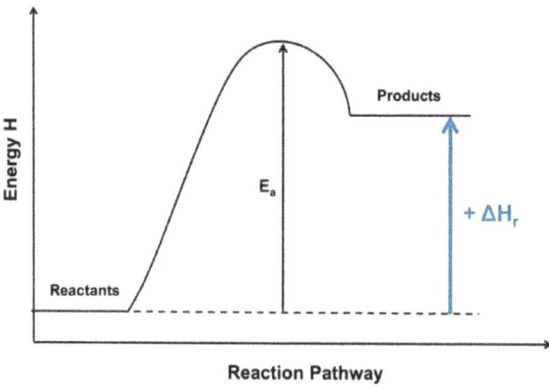

Make sure arrows point in the correct direction and everything is labelled.

Paper 2 (8462)
Topic 6 – The Rate and Extent of Chemical Change

Rates of Reactions & Catalyst

Rates depend on... (four points)

Definition & equation of rate of reaction

Collision theory (four points)

Definition of catalyst

Two properties of catalysts

Enzymes

Exothermic energy profile diagram with and without catalyst

Rates of Reactions

Rates (speed) depend on
- temperature
- surface area (size of particles)
- catalyst
- concentrations of reactants (or pressure for gases)

Rate of reaction: change of amount of product or reactant over time t

$$r = \frac{\Delta m}{\Delta t}$$

Δm: change of mass (or volume, moles etc.) [g]
Δt: change of time [s]

Collision Theory
- Higher temperature -> particles higher speed => more successful collisions
- Higher concentration -> more frequent collisions
- Larger surface area -> particles can access more area and more frequent collisions
- Catalyst -> see below

Catalyst

Definition: Increases rate of reaction by **lowering activation energy** (more successful collisions) and providing an **alternative reaction pathway**. Catalysts are **not used up** during the reactions.

- **Does not change chemical equilibrium**
- Catalysts **save energy** and costs by lowering reaction temperature: Fe in Haber process
- **Enzymes** are **biological catalysts** in organisms

Exothermic Energy Profile Diagram with and without Catalyst

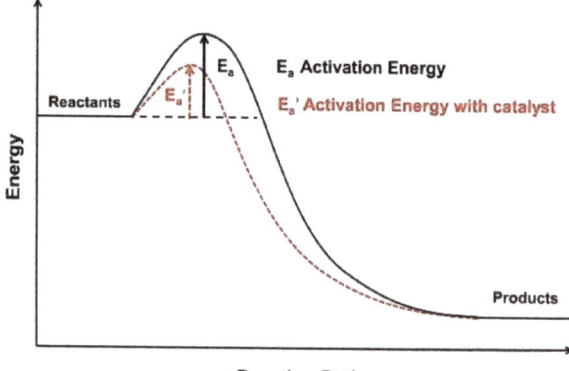

Measuring Rates of Reaction

Five Methods

Six steps for measuring rates of reaction of Mg with HCl

Reaction equation

Graphs for two concentrations of HCl and larger amount of Mg

Description of the three graphs

Measuring Rates of Reaction (Practical)

Methods
- Precipitation: measure time until marker disappears.
  HCl + sodium thiosulfate => $S_{(s)\ yellow}$ + $SO_{2(g)}$ *(toxic!)*
  -> increase of HCl concentration increases rate and reduces time until yellow precipitate appears
- Change in mass when gas given off (balance, most accurate)
- Volume of gas given off (syringe in sealed system; or upside down water-filled measuring cylinder -> less accurate => gas can dissolve)
- Measure time until change of colour of a solution (subjective)

Measuring rates of reaction of magnesium with hydrochloric acid
- A conical flask with a set volume of dilute HCl is placed on a balance
- A specific mass of magnesium ribbon is added to the flask which is plugged with cotton wool (prevents acid spitting out)
- A stopwatch is started and the mass is recorded at regular intervals
- Calculate the mass lost for each time point and create a table
- Plot a graph with the masses lost (y-axis) against time (x-axis)
- Repeat with a more concentrated acid solution while keeping the other variables (mass of Mg, volume of HCl) the same.

Reaction: $Mg_{(s)}$ + $2HCl_{(aq)}$ -> $MgCl_{2(aq)}$ + $H_{2(g)}$

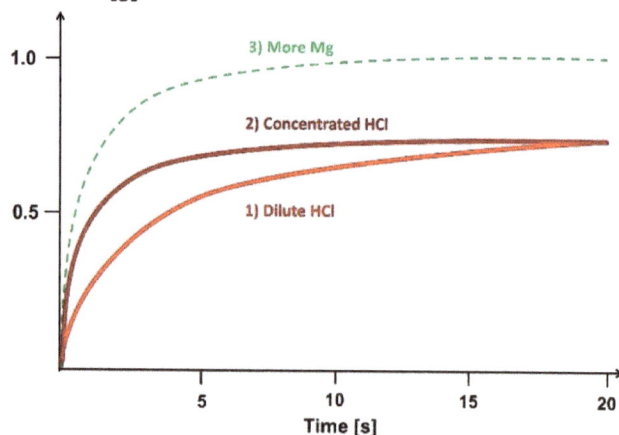

1) **Original reaction with dilute HCl**
2) **Faster reaction with more concentrated HCl -> steeper graph**
=> both graphs converge at the same level, because same amount of Mg is used
3) **Reaction with dilute HCl but larger amount of Mg.** Increasing the other reactant results in a faster reaction and higher level but should not be done in a series of experiment where only one reactant (acid concentration) is changed.

Calculating Rates of Reaction

Calculate mean rate of whole reaction from graph
Calculate mean rate between two time points with slope equation
Example graph of calculating mean rate

Calculate rate at particular time point of a curved graph
Example graph at time point 0 s
Four steps of the tangent method

Calculate Rates of Reaction

I) Calculate mean rate from a graph

- If calculating the mean rate of the whole reaction, choose the time point where the graph starts to go flat as final point (15 s).
- Use the slope equation ($m = \Delta y / \Delta x$) to calculate the mean rate of a curved graph between two time points or the gradient of a linear graph:

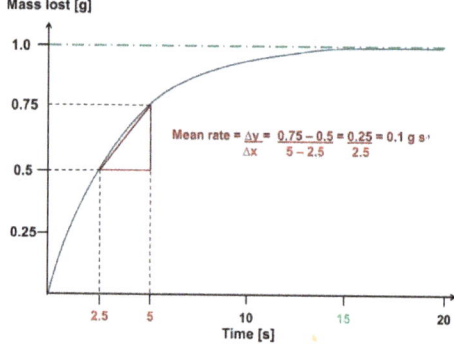

II) Calculate the rate at a particular time point of a curved graph

- Calculate the gradient of the tangent at this point to get the rate

Example: draw tangent through mass point at 0 s in graph below

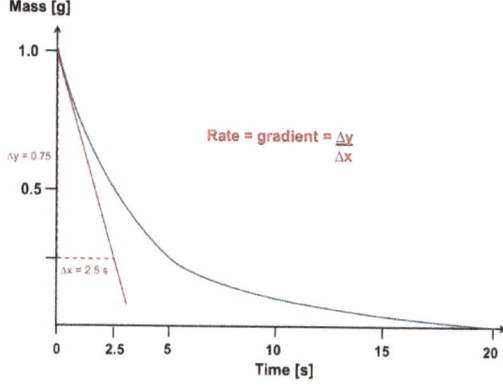

-> can also choose any other time point t and draw tangent through it.
-> pick two points on the tangent, so that their Y and X values are easy to read and their differences are large.
-> calculate the $\Delta y / \Delta x$ values for these points.
-> put these values into the slope equation to get the rate:
Gradient m = rate = $0.75 / 2.5 = 0.3$ g s^{-1}

Equilibrium and Reversible Reactions

Definition of reversible reaction

Definition for dynamic equilibrium (four points)

Two equilibrium scenarios affecting yield

Three conditions affecting the equilibrium position

Effect of catalyst on chemical equilibrium

Le Chetallier's Principle

Haber process with changes of conditions (pressure, heat, conc.)

Tip

Equilibrium and Reversible Reactions

Reversible reaction: products convert back to reactants (reaction goes both ways) -> incomplete reaction => draw double arrow: ⇌

Dynamic equilibrium
- **Rates of the forward and reverse reactions are equal**
- Both reactions still going on: **in balance** => low percentage of product
- **Concentrations** of reactants and products remain **constant**
- Only in **closed system** (reactants or products cannot enter or leave)

Important for yield in chemical industry
- Equilibrium lies to the right: concentration of products greater than reactants -> high yield
- Equilibrium lies to the left: concentration of products smaller than reactants -> low yield

-> First scenario is favoured by chemical industry, which wants as much product as possible (high yield)

Conditions affecting the equilibrium position
- Temperature
- Concentration of reactants and products
- Pressure (for gases)

=> **Catalyst does not change equilibrium** but increases **rate of both reactions (equilibrium is reached faster)**

Le Chetallier's Principle: When the conditions of a system at equilibrium changes, the position of the equilibrium shifts in the direction that opposes (counteracts) the change
-> predicts the effect of changes to an equilibrium system (reaction)

Example:
Ammonia manufacture (Haber-process): iron catalyst, 200 atm, 450 C

$$N_{2(g)} + 3H_{2(g)} \rightleftharpoons 2NH_{3(g)} \qquad \text{exothermic}$$

+ pressure -> shifts to the side with less moles of gases (here to the right: 2 < 4)
+ heat   -> shifts in the direction of endothermic process (here to left)
+ concentration reactants -> shifts to right
− concentration products -> shifts to right

Tip: Highlight the direction of the endothermic reaction in the equation. Temperature increase will shift the equilibrium in this direction.
Temperature decrease will shift it in the opposite direction.

Topic 7 – Organic Chemistry

Alkanes

Definition of alkanes

Reactivity

Homologues series with general formula and physical states

Displayed formulae of the first three alkanes

Description of displayed formula

Description of molecular formula

Definition of homologues series

With increased chain length... (three points)

Applications (two points)

Preparation

Tip

Alkanes

Saturated hydrocarbons (only single C-C bonds, only hydrogen and carbon)

-> unreactive

Homologues series of alkanes: $C_n H_{2n+2}$

    Methane, Ethane, Propane, Butane   -> flammable gases
    Pentane, *Hexane, Heptane, Octane*   -> liquids

```
      H              H   H           H   H   H
      |              |   |           |   |   |
   H—C—H          H—C—C—H         H—C—C—C—H
      |              |   |           |   |   |
      H              H   H           H   H   H
```

  Methane (1 C atom)   Ethane (2 C)   Propane (3 C)

Displayed formula: shows all covalent bonds as lines
Molecular formula: shows number of atoms of each element: C_2H_6 (ethane)

Homologues series: a group of compounds with the same general formula and the same functional group -> **similar reactions** *(they differ by a 'CH$_2$' group)*

With increased chain length:
- more viscous (gloopy)
- higher boiling points (less volatile) due to greater intermolecular forces
- less flammable

Applications
- Fuel: cars etc.
- Short chain hydrocarbons: bottled gases (liquid under pressure)

Preparation
- from crude oil

==Tip: Carbon has always four bonds==

Crude Oil – Fuel

Origin and properties of crude oil (two points)

Separation of crude oil fractions by... (two points)

List of six fractions

Cracking

Catalytic cracking

Steam cracking

Three applications

Complete combustion with O_2 with equation and side products

Incomplete combustion with two products

Crude Oil – Fuel

- crude oil is a **non-renewable, finite, fossil fuel**: formed from plankton, plants and animals over millions of years under high pressure and temperature. Drilled up to the surface.
- crude oil consists of hydrocarbons (alkanes) with different chain length.
- the temperature gradient of the **fractionating column** separates these into different fractions, according to their boiling point by **fractional distillation:** heating -> vaporisation (gas), then cooling in tower -> condensation (liquid)
- the longer the chain the higher the boiling point (bottom of fractionating column).

Different fractions

<RT	Gases	$C_1 - C_4$	LPG, camping gas
< 40 C	Petrol	$C_5 - C_{12}$	petrol
<180 C	Kerosene	$C_{12} - C_{15}$	jet fuel
<250 C	Diesel	$C_{15} - C_{30}$	diesel for lorries, central heating
<340 C	Heavy Fuel Oil	$C_{30} - C_{50}$	lubricating, power stations
>350 C	Bitumen	C_{50+}	road, roofing

Cracking
Long chains (gloopy tar) are **broken down** by cracking (thermal decomposition) to produce smaller chains and **alkenes** -> More demand for fuels & alkenes

Catalytic Cracking
Thermal decomposition with hot catalyst Al_2O_3

Steam Cracking
Thermal decomposition of alkanes mixed with steam at high temperature
$C_{10}H_{22}$ -> C_8H_{18} + C_2H_4
Alkane   shorter alkane   **alkene**

Applications
- Fuel for transport (cars)
- Feedstock for petrochemical industry: polymers, solvents, detergents
- Organic compounds

Complete combustion with O_2: produces $CO_2 + H_2O$
$$CH_4 + 2O_2 -> CO_2 + 2H_2O$$
-> Side products nitrogen oxides NO_x (toxic) in car engines (high temperature)
-> Catalytic converter (platinum) in car: $2NO -> N_2 + O_2$
-> Fuel contains **sulphur** which is oxidised to SO_2. This causes pollution:
=> Respiratory problems
=> Acid rain: SO_2 or NO_x mix with clouds to form H_2SO_4 or HNO_3 respectively

Incomplete combustion with limited supply of O_2: produces $CO + H_2O$
- Carbon monoxide (colourless, no smell, poisonous: blocks haemoglobin)
- Soot (Carbon particles) -> reflect sunlight => global dimming

Alkenes

Definition
Reactivity
General formula
Naming
Reactions of double bond
Reactions of alkenes:
Addition of halogens with reaction equation
Test for alkenes
Hydrogenation with word equation
Steam hydration with word equation
Application
Complete combustion
Incomplete combustion with reaction equation

Alkenes

Definitions: Unsaturated hydrocarbons (C=C double bonds) -> **reactive**

General Formula: C_nH_{2n} (two fewer H than Alkanes)

Naming

$$H_3C-\underset{1}{CH}=\underset{2}{CH}-\underset{3}{CH}_3$$

C_2H_4 — Ethene (2 C)
C_3H_6 — Propene (3 C)
C_4H_8 — Butene (4 C)
C_5H_{10} — Pentene (5 C)

Double bond: Addition reactions

Addition of Halogens (X_2: F_2, Cl_2, Br_2, I_2)

Alkene (ethene) + X_2 -> Halogenoalkane (dibromoethane)

-> bromine (**brown-red**) gets decolourised

Test for alkenes:
- Shake with bromine water at RT: orange -> colourless

Hydrogenation – Addition of hydrogen with catalyst *(Ni)*
Alkene + H_2 -> Alkane

Steam Hydration – Addition of water with catalyst *(Phosphoric Acid)*
Alkene + H_2O -> Alcohol
-> unreacted ethene is separated in a condenser and recycled back into reactor

Application
Polymers/plastics

Combustion Reactions

Complete combustion
Burning with O_2 produces CO_2 + H_2O (see revision card 'Alkanes')

Incomplete combustion
produces CO (Carbon monoxide - poisonous) or C (soot – lung damage)
=> **smoky yellow flame** (less energy released)
$$C_4H_8 + 5O_2 -> 2CO + 2CO_2 + 4H_2O$$

Addition Polymers & Functional Groups

Definition of polymer
Reaction equation to form poly(propene)
Rules for equation (three points)
Characteristics of reaction (two points)
Naming with two examples

Definition of functional group
Alkane
Alkene
Alcohol
Carboxylic acid
Ester

Addition Polymers

Definition of polymers: Long chain molecules of monomers *(poly – many)*

$$n \; \underset{\substack{\text{Propene -> alkene} \\ \text{Monomer}}}{\text{CH}_3\text{-CH=CH}_2} \longrightarrow \underset{\substack{\text{Poly(propene) -> alkane} \\ \text{Repeating unit}}}{\left[\text{-CH(CH}_3\text{)-CH}_2\text{-} \right]_n}$$

Rules
- draw square bracket through middle of bond
- polymer chain is built only from carbons with a double bond -> **all other carbons form side chains**
- remember to put 'n' on both sides of equation

Reaction characteristics
- **addition polymerization** (high pressure, catalyst)
- 100 % atom economy (no waste products)

Name from monomer

Poly(ethene): cheap, strong, moulded => bags, bottles, bowls
*Poly(propene) – **strong fibres, high elasticity** => **crates, robes, carpets***

Functional groups

Definition: Group of atoms in a molecule which is responsible for the reaction

R (residue): alkyl-group C_nH_{2n+1}: -CH_3 (methyl), -C_2H_5 (ethyl), -C_3H_7 (propyl),...

Alkane	R-CH_3
Alkene	R—CH=CH—R
Alcohol	R-OH
Carboxylic Acid	R—C(=O)—OH
Ester	R^1—C(=O)—O—R^2

Alcohols

Functional group of alcohols

Genera formula

Homologous series with first four alcohols

Naming

Reactions of alcohols with:

Sodium

Oxygen to form...

Oxygen (combustion)

Carboxylic acids to form...

Two methods to prepare ethanol

Conditions for fermentation (four points)

Four applications of alcohols

Alcohols

R-OH   **General Formula:** $C_nH_{2n+1}OH$

Homologous Series

| CH_3OH | C_2H_5OH | C_3H_7OH | C_4H_9OH |
| Methanol | Ethanol | Propanol | Butanol |

Naming: Replace the 'e' of the Alkane with 'ol'

Reactions

with sodium
$2C_2H_5OH + 2Na \rightarrow 2C_2H_5ONa + H_2$
ethanol + sodium -> *sodium ethoxide* + hydrogen

with oxygen (oxidising agent) to form carboxylic acid
$C_2H_5OH + O_2 \rightarrow CH_3COOH + H_2O$
ethanol   ethanoic acid

with oxygen (combustion)
$C_2H_5OH + 3O_2 \rightarrow \mathbf{2CO_2 + 3H_2O}$
Ethanol + oxygen -> **carbon dioxide + water**

with carboxylic acids to form esters
$CH_3CH_2COOH + C_2H_5OH \rightarrow CH_3CH_2COOC_2H_5 + H_2O$
Propanoic acid + ethanol ->   ester   + water
-> see revision card 'Carboxylic Acids'

Preparation of Ethanol

I) Steam Hydration
-> see revision card 'Alkenes'

II) Fermentation

Fermentation reaction: Sugar $(C_6H_{12}O_6)$ -> $\mathbf{2C_2H_5OH} + 2CO_2$

Conditions for fermentation
- yeast
- Anaerobic (no oxygen)
- Slightly acidic
- Correct Temperature: around 37°C

Applications: drinks (beer, wine), solvent for oils and fats *(non-polar)*, plastics, fuel (burns cleanly in spirit burner)

Carboxylic Acids

Drawing of functional group

Homologous series with naming of the first four

Important property of carboxylic acids

Reactions with:

metals

carbonates

bases

alcohols

Preparation

Carboxylic acids

$$R-C(=O)-OH$$

Homologous Series

HCOOH	CH_3COOH	CH_3CH_2COOH	$CH_3CH_2CH_2COOH$
methanoic acid	ethanoic acid	propanoic acid	butanoic acid

They are weak Acids (higher pH):

Reactions

with metals (redox)
$2Na + 2CH_3COOH \rightarrow 2CH_3COONa + H_2$
metal + carboxylic acid -> sodium ethanoate (salt) + hydrogen

with carbonates (neutralisation)
$CaCO_3 + 2CH_3COOH \rightarrow (CH_3COO)_2Ca + CO_2 + H_2O$
carbonate + carboxylic acid -> salt + carbon dioxide + water

with bases (neutralisation)
$CaO + 2CH_3COOH \rightarrow (CH_3COO)_2Ca + H_2O$
base + carboxylic acid -> salt + water

=> same reactions as inorganic acids -> see revision card 'acids'

Ester formation

$H_3C-C(=O)-OH$ + $HO-CH_3$ $\underset{}{\overset{H_2SO_4 \text{ conc}}{\rightleftharpoons}}$ $H_3C-C(=O)-O-CH_3$ + H_2O

| carboxylic acid | + | alcohol | ⇌ | Ester | + | water |
| ethanoic acid | + | methanol | | methyl ethanoate | | |

-> acid catalyst (H_2SO_4)

Preparation
- Oxidation of ethanol to ethanoic acid (wine gone bad -> vinegar)

Condensation Polymers

Condensation polymerization (two points)
Preparation of polypeptides with equations
Circling method
Definition of protein
Functions of proteins
Preparation of polyesters with equations
Definition of Diol
Drawing lines method
Both functional groups on same molecule
Tip how to recognise an addition polymer
DNA
Sugars

Condensation Polymers

Condensation polymerization
- **Monomers form a polymer and another small molecule (H_2O)**
- Monomers must have two functional groups

Polypeptide
amino acid (glycine) + amino acid   ->   poly-peptide   +   water

=> Circle atoms which form the water. The leftover half-bonds form the peptide bonds.
Proteins: Long-chain polypeptides made from different amino acids
Functions: Enzymes – biological catalysts, Haemoglobin – oxygen transport, Antibodies – immune system, body tissue

Polyester
dicarboxylic acid   +   diol   ->   poly-ester   +   water

Diol: Compound with two alcohol (-OH) groups

To determine monomers from a chain (repeat unit):
draw lines through the middle of the ester bonds and add water (OH, H) to CO and O respectively to get the structural formula of the monomer

Carboxylic acid and alcohol group on same molecule -> poly-ester + water

Tip: If the polymer chain (repeat unit) is not connected by peptide or ester groups, but C-C single bonds, then it is an addition polymer -> see rev. card

DNA: Nucleotide polymer which stores genetic information for growth.
Monomers -> nucleotides which contain four different **bases**: A, C, G, T
The bases cross link two polymer chains together to form a double helix structure. Their order codes for genes

Carbohydrate polymers: from sugars -> **starch** (energy), **cellulose** (cell wall)

Topic 8 – Chemical Analysis

Purity and Formulations
&
Chromatography

Definition of pure substance
Definition of mixture
Definition of formulation
Three applications of formulations
Tests for purity (three points)

Function of chromatography
Two causes for separation
The two phases of paper chromatography
Five steps of paper chromatography
Equation for R_f value

Purity and Formulations

Pure Substance: contains only one compound or element

Mixture: of different elements or compounds, not chemically bonded together
-> parts can be separated by physical methods

Formulation: Mixture with exact amounts (measured quantities) of components, which contribute to the required function -> follows a recipe (formula) and has a precise purpose

Applications of formulations: Pharmaceutical drugs (deliver the right concentration of the drug to the correct organ), cleaning products & cosmetics

Tests for Purity
- A pure substance has a specific melting and boiling point, which can be compared to literature values (data book). Impurities lower melting point.
- **Measuring the melting point:** the solid is slowly heated in a capillary tube, in a beaker of oil containing a thermometer; the temperature is read when the solid melts.
- **Measuring the boiling point:** use a distillation apparatus.

Chromatography

-> Separating and identifying components of a mixture by degree of interaction with the stationary phase:
- Separation due to different **interactions with stationary phase (solid or thick liquid)**
- or different **solubility in mobile phase (liquid or gas)** -> equilibrium

Paper Chromatography
- **Stationary phase:** solid filter paper
- **Mobile phase:** liquid solvent (alcohol, ester)
- Spots of the mixture and reference substances are put on a pencil line at the lower edge of the plate (starting point, baseline)
- The different steps are described on revision card 'Separation Techniques'
- Mark the position of the solvent front with pencil after endpoint is reached
- Measure distance from the pencil baseline (start) to the middle of the spot (a) and the solvent front line (x)
- Compare R_f value of the unknown component with that of the known/pure compound (reference)

R_f value:

$$R_f = \frac{a}{x}$$

a: distance moved by solute (compound) in cm
x: distance moved by solvent in cm
R_f: *Retardation Factor*

Tests for Gases
&
Tests for Anions

Tests for:

Chlorine

Oxygen

Carbon dioxide

Hydrogen

Tests for:

Carbonate

Sulphates

Halides

Workings of precipitation reactions (two points)

Tests for Gases (Practical)

Chlorine
Bleaches damp, red litmus paper white

Oxygen
Relights glowing splint

Carbon dioxide (limewater test)
$Ca(OH)_{2(aq)} + CO_{2(g)} \rightarrow CaCO_{3(s)} + H_2O_{(l)}$
-> bubble CO_2 through a calcium hydroxide solution (**limewater**)
=> limewater turns **milky/cloudy (precipitation)** in presence of CO_2

Hydrogen
Squeaky pop when lit with a lighted splint

Tests for Anions

Carbonates: $CO_3^{2-}{}_{(aq)} + 2H^+{}_{(aq)} \rightarrow H_2O_{(l)} + CO_{2(g)}$ fizzing, **carbonate disappears**
-> add dilute acid to carbonate
-> combine with test for CO_2 (see above)
-> see revision card 'Bases'

Sulphates: $Ba^{2+}{}_{(aq)} + SO_4^{2-}{}_{(aq)} \rightarrow BaSO_{4(s)}$ **white precipitate**
-> add $BaCl_2$ solution and HCl
=> acid removes carbonates, which could precipitate

Halides: $Ag^+{}_{(aq)} + X^-{}_{(aq)} \rightarrow AgX_{(s)}$ precipitate
X^-: halide ion (Cl^-, Br^-, I^-)
-> add acidified **$AgNO_3$** solution (**HNO_3** -> removes carbonates & sulphates)

Halide (X^-)	Precipitate
F^-	-
Cl^-	white
Br^-	cream
I^-	yellow

Workings of precipitation reactions:
- Some salts are more soluble than others
- Soluble salts stay in solution, insoluble salts precipitate out when formed

Tests for Cations
&
Flame Emission Spectroscopy

Method for flame tests (three points)
Colours for Li^+, Na^+, K^+, Ca^{2+}, Cu^{2+}

Workings of flame emission spectroscopy:
How light is emitted (three points)
Properties and applications of the spectrum (three points)
Relationship between spectrum and concentration (one point)
Advantages of spectrum to flame tests (two points)
Advantages of instrumental methods (three points)

Chemical tests for Ca^{2+}, Fe^{2+}, Fe^{3+}, Cu^{2+}, Al^{3+} ions

Tests for Cations (Practical)

Flame Tests
Method
- Clean platinum- or nichrome-wire by dipping it into HCl and holding it in Bunsen burner blue flame until flame becomes colourless.
- Pick up some salt crystals and hold them into blue Bunsen flame.
- Electrons get elevated by heat energy. They emit coloured light when falling back to original energy level.

Colours
Li^+ crimson red
Na^+ bright yellow -> *can mask other colours*
K^+ lilac
Ca^{2+} orange red
Cu^{2+} green

Flame Emission Spectroscopy

- Ions of an aqueous sample are heat up in a flame.
- Their electrons move from ground state to excited state (higher shell).
- When falling back light is emitted which is separated by its wavelengths in a spectroscope.
- The emitted wavelengths are characteristic for each element.
- A set of coloured lines is seen on a black background -> **line spectrum**.
- This pattern is used to identify the ions.
- The intensity of the emitted light allows to calculate their concentrations.
- In contrast to flame tests also components of a mixtures can be identified: the spectrum of the mixture is a combination of spectra of the components.
- In flame tests the colours would mix => only suitable for single metal

Advantages of Instrumental Methods
- Very accurate
- very sensitive
- Very fast

Chemical Tests for Metal Ions

Precipitation reactions with NaOH solution
$Ca^{2+}_{(aq)} + 2OH^-_{(aq)} \rightarrow Ca(OH)_{2(s)}$ **white precipitate**
$Fe^{2+}_{(aq)} + 2OH^-_{(aq)} \rightarrow Fe(OH)_{2(s)}$ green precipitate
$Fe^{3+}_{(aq)} + 3OH^-_{(aq)} \rightarrow Fe(OH)_{3(s)}$ red-brown/rust prec.
$Cu^{2+}_{(aq)} + 2OH^-_{(aq)} \rightarrow Cu(OH)_{2(s)}$ blue precipitate
$Al^{3+}_{(aq)} + 3OH^-_{(aq)} \rightarrow Al(OH)_{3(s)}$ **white precipitate**
$Al(OH)_3$ redissolves in excess NaOH -> colourless solution

Topic 9 – Chemistry of the Atmosphere

The Atmosphere

Composition of the atmosphere (three points)

Evolution of the atmosphere:
Phase 1 (four points)
Phase 2 (four points)
Phase 3 (three points)

Changes in the atmosphere through human activity (four points)

The Atmosphere

Composition
- ~ **80% N_2** nitrogen
- ~ **20% O_2** oxygen
- ~ **1% CO_2** carbon dioxide, noble gases & water vapour

Evolution of the atmosphere in the past 4.6 billion years:

Phase 1 – Volcanoes release gases
- Earth surface very hot, slowly cooled down.
- Erupting **volcanoes** released gases: CO_2, CH_4, N_2, H_2O.
- Early atmosphere: **no oxygen** but mostly CO_2.
- When water vapour condensed **oceans** were formed.

Phase 2 – Absorption of carbon dioxide
- CO_2 was removed by dissolving in the ocean forming **carbonate precipitates** -> sediments on the seabed.
- **Green plants** and **algae** evolved. They used up CO_2 and produced O_2 through photosynthesis.
- Marine animals, e.g. shell fish used CO_2 to build their **shells** ($CaCO_3$).
- When the plants and animals died they were buried by layers of rock/sand and compressed into **coal (plants) and oil (plankton)** -> **fossil fuels**

Phase 3 – Production of oxygen
- Plants and algae produced oxygen through **photosynthesis** by converting CO_2 and water into sugars (~ 2.7 billion years ago).
  $6CO_2 + 6H_2O + \text{light} \rightarrow C_6H_{12}O_6 \text{ (glucose)} + 6O_2$
- With Oxygen present more **complex organisms** like animals developed.
- Around **200 million** years ago the atmosphere reached a composition similar to that of today.

-> difficult to get evidence of a process which took very long so long ago.

Current changes in the atmosphere through human activity
- **Burning fossil fuel** (car/power stations) releases locked up carbon and increases CO_2 content.
- **Farm animals** and decomposition of waste produce **methane**.
- Methane and CO_2 are greenhouse gases which causes **global warming**
- **Deforestation** also contributes to increased CO_2 levels
  -> less CO_2 removed through photosynthesis.

The Greenhouse Effect

Three greenhouse gases
Mechanism of the greenhouse effect (three points)
Scientific evidence for global warming (three points)
Effect of climate change (four points)
Carbon footprints (two points)
Reducing carbon footprints:
Four ways of reducing carbon footprints
Three obstacles for reducing carbon footprints

The Greenhouse Effect

Greenhouse gases
- H_2O, CO_2, CH_4
- do not absorb incoming short wavelength radiation
- absorb outgoing long wavelength IR radiation -> thermal radiation

Mechanism of the greenhouse effect
- Earth absorbs UV/visible light (short wavelengths) from the sun and heats up
- Heat is usually radiated back into space as long wavelength IR radiation.
- Greenhouse gases in atmosphere absorb IR frequencies and re-emit them back to earth causing global warming (rise of sea levels, climate change)

Scientific evidence for global warming
- Average temperature of earth surface increased
- Evidence has been peer-reviewed and is reliable
- However, this is still disputed by some media due to the complexity of the climate

Effect of climate change (global warming)
- Ice caps melting causes rise in sea levels, coastal flooding and erosion
- Change in rainfall pattern causes draughts and floods for farmers
- More storms
- Wild life affected

Carbon footprints
- A measure of the amount of greenhouse gases releases over the life cycle of a product (impossible to measure)
- Usually just rough calculations because many factors have to be taken into account

Methods of reducing carbon footprints
- Use of renewable energy sources instead of fossil fuels
- Conserving energy through fuel efficiency and cutting waste
- Taxing cars and industries (licences) according to CO_2 emissions
- Capturing and underground storage of CO_2 (old oil wells)

Obstacles for reducing carbon footprints
- These changes might reduce economic growth
- Not easy to get international agreements
- Not easy to get people to change their life style

Topic 10 – Using Resources

Materials and their Properties

Definition of ceramics
Clay ceramic with applications
Two types of glass
Three properties of ceramics

Definition of composites
Fiberglass with properties and applications
Carbon fibre with properties and applications
Concrete with properties and applications
Properties of composites

Properties of polymers depend on…
Two types of poly(ethene) with properties and applications
Thermosoftening and thermosetting
Three properties of polymers

Materials and their Properties

Ceramics

-> non-metal solids from non-carbon-based compounds with high melting points

Clay ceramic: Soft clay out of the ground is moulded and hardened (fired) at high temperatures -> pottery, porcelain, bricks

Glass: Mixture of limestone, sand and sodium carbonate is melted, moulded and then cooled again -> **Soda-lime glass** (transparent)
Borosilicate glass is made from sand and boron trioxide and has a higher melting point -> laboratory glassware (transparent)

Properties of ceramics:
- Insulators of heat and electricity
- Brittle
- Stiff

Composites

-> one material (fibres, fragments as reinforcement) embedded in another (matrix binder) => **two different materials**

Fiberglass: glass fibres in a polymer matrix
-> low density and very strong => skis, boats, surfboards

Carbon fibre: carbon fibres or nanotubes in a polymer matrix
-> light and very strong => aeroplanes, sport cars

Concrete: sand and gravel (aggregate) embedded in cement
-> very strong => building material (houses)

Properties of composites:
- depend on the reinforcement and the matrix used -> many different uses

Polymers -> see rev. cards 'Addition Polymers' and 'Condensation Polymers'

Their properties depend on the **monomer, catalyst** and the **reaction conditions**:

LD Low density poly(ethene) is made from ethene at moderate temperature under high pressure with a catalyst -> flexible => bags, bottles

HD High density poly(ethene) is made from ethene at lower temperature and lower pressure with a different catalyst -> more rigid => water tanks, pipes

Thermosoftening: weak forces between individual chains => melt, remould

Thermosetting: cross-links between chains -> hard, solid, rigid => do not melt

Properties of polymers:
- Insulators of heat and electricity
- Flexible
- Easily moulded

Metals & Corrosion

Four properties of metals

Three applications of metals

Definition of alloys with properties

Definition of steel

Three types of steel

Bronze

Brass

Gold alloys

Aluminium alloys

Definition of corrosion

Rusting with word equation

Properties of rust

Three types of corrosion prevention

Corrosion of aluminium (two points)

Metals

-> see revision card 'Metallic Bonding'

Properties of metals
- good electrical & thermal conductors: free moving electrons
- malleable: layers can slide
- ductile: can be drawn into wires
- shiny and soft -> only alloys are hard

Applications: wires, car bodies, cutlery

Alloys

Definition: Mixtures of different metals or a metal and a non-metal (C)
-> different sized atoms distort the layers, preventing them sliding => harder

Steel: Alloy of iron with different metals and different content of carbon
Low carbon steel: $0.1 - 0.3\%$ carbon, easily shaped -> car bodies
High carbon steel: $0.22 - 2.5\%$ carbon, strong, brittle -> construction
Stainless steel: Chromium & nickel, corrosion-resistant, hard -> cutlery

Bronze: Copper & tin, hard -> medals, statues

Brass: Copper & zinc, malleable, low friction -> water taps, door fittings

Gold: 24 carats pure (soft); jewellery: zinc/copper/silver alloys, 18 carats (75 %)

Aluminium alloys: low density -> aircraft

Corrosion

Definition: metals are destroyed by reacting with substances in the environment

Rusting

-> corrosion of iron: **iron + oxygen + water -> hydrated iron(III) oxide**

Rust: soft crumbly solid which flakes off -> iron is destroyed
Both **air and water** need to be present for rusting to occur
-> proven by experiments

Corrosion prevention
- **Barriers** for O_2/H_2O: Paints, Plastic coating, Oiling/Greasing
- **Electroplating:** coating with a different metal by electrolysis
- **Zinc coating: sacrificial metal** with lower potential -> galvanising

Aluminium
- Reacts with air to form an aluminium oxide layer which does not flake.
- This oxide layer prevents further corrosion -> less corrosion than iron.

Finite and Renewable Resources
&
Reuse and Recycling

Definition of natural resources
Definition of man-made resources
Definition of renewable resources
Definition of finite resources (two points)

Definition of sustainability
Two points about sustainability and finite resources
Improving sustainability (four points)

Definition of life cycle assessment
Four stages of the life of a product

Finite and Renewable Resources

Natural Resources
-> they form without human input and come from the earth, sea or air: cotton, oil

Man-Made Resources
-> synthetic products like plastics (replace natural products like rubber)

Renewable Resources
-> reform at a similar or faster rate than being used up: timber, food

Finite (non-renewable) Resources
-> reform too slow to get replaced: fossil fuels, uranium, ores
- need to be extracted and to undergo man-made processes: fractional distillation, reduction of ores
- the social, economic and environmental effects of extraction have to be balanced, e.g. mining provides jobs, but is bad for the environment (destroys habitats, uses energy, produces waste)

Reuse and Recycling

Sustainability
-> Needs of the present generation should not damage the needs of future generations
- continued use of finite resources is unsustainable
- extracting and processing resources can also be unsustainable when using energy from finite resources

Improving sustainability
- Using fewer finite resources
- Developing and adapting processes to use less resources and energy -> catalyst
- Recycling metals by melting & casting saves energy and reduces waste
- Recycling glass by reusing bottles or melting and reshaping after colour separation into glass wool for insulation

Life Cycle Assessments
-> assesses impact of a product through every stage of its life, e.g. its use of energy, resources and its production of waste and pollution

I) Raw materials: extracting and processing needs energy and causes damage to the environment
II) Manufacture and Packaging: use of energy, pollution and disposal of waste
III) Using the Product: fertilisers can pollute water.
Lifespan of product very important: The longer the life span the less waste.
IV) Disposal: landfill sites can pollute land and water. Incineration causes air pollution

Potable Water

Definition of potable water
Definition of pure water
Definition of fresh water
Three sources of drinking water
Four steps of drinking water treatment
Waste water treatment (three points)
Five stages of sewage treatment
Application of recycled waste water

Potable Water

Definition: Drinking water which is safe to drink or has been treated. It contains the right level of dissolved salts and a pH 6.5 – 8.5

Pure Water: contains only H_2O (no salts)

Fresh Water: water with not much salt dissolved (e.g. rain water)

Sources of drinking water:
- Surface water (lakes, rivers, reservoirs)
- Groundwater (stored in aquifers)
- Desalination of sea water (Kuwait):
    - Distillation of sea water (high energy consumption)
    - Reverse osmosis through membranes (larger salt ions cannot pass membrane)

Drinking water treatment:
1. Filtration through mesh removes twigs.
2. Then passed through sand & gravel bed to remove solids.
3. Sterilisation with chlorine, ozone or ultraviolet light (UV) to kill harmful bacteria.
4. Sometimes addition of fluoride to prevent tooth decay (controversial).

Waste water treatment
- Sewers deliver waste water (toilet, slurry) to sewage treatment plants
- They remove organic matter and harmful microbes to prevent pollution and health risks before feeding it back into freshwater sources
- Industrial waste water has to have additional treatment stages to remove harmful chemicals

Sewage Treatment stages
1. Screening: removal of large chunks of material (twigs etc.)
2. Sedimentation: heavier solids sink to the bottom of settlement tanks to form sludge
3. Aerobic digestion: aerobic bacteria digest organic matter of the effluent while oxygen is pumped through
4. Anaerobic digestion: Sludge is broken down by anaerobic bacteria releasing methane (energy source) -> left over waste is used as fertiliser
5. Additional stages: only necessary when toxic substances present
    –> adding chemicals, UV radiation, membranes

=> recycled waste water can be used as drinking water (low energy consumption but more processes than desalination)

The Haber Process
&
NPK Fertilisers

Reaction equation for the Haber process
Sources for the reactants
Conditions of the Haber process:
Temperature
Pressure
Catalyst
Apparatus used in Haber process
Application for ammonia

Four reasons for using NPK fertilisers
Production of ammonium nitrate (three points)
Sourcing of potassium
Sourcing and processing of phosphate

The Haber Process

-> see revision card 'Equilibrium and Reversible Reactions'

$$N_{2(g)} + 3H_{2(g)} \rightleftharpoons 2NH_{3(g)} \quad \text{exothermic}$$

Reactants: N_2 from liquefied air, H_2 from reacting methane with steam

Conditions: iron catalyst, 200 atm, 450 °C
- → temperature of 450 °C is a compromise between yield of dynamic equilibrium (lower temperature preferred) and rate (higher temperature)
- → pressure of 200 atm is also compromise: higher pressure would be too expensive and too dangerous
- → iron catalyst just increases rate, but does not affect yield

Apparatus: condenser liquefies the ammonia, unused N_2 & H_2 are recycled back

Application: ammonia (NH_3) is used to make ammonium nitrate -> fertiliser

NPK Fertilisers

- Growing crops deplete the soil from important nutrients
- The three most important elements in these nutrients are nitrogen (**N**), phosphorus (**P**) and potassium (**K**)
- They need to be replaced by using manure or synthetic (formulated) fertilisers to increase crop yield.
- Formulated fertilisers do not smell and have the correct percentage of nutrients

Sourcing

- **Ammonia** from the Haber process is oxidised to nitric acid
- Ammonia and nitric acid form **ammonium nitrate**:
  $NH_3 + HNO_3 \rightarrow NH_4NO_3$
- In the lab lower concentrations of reactants and different steps (titration & crystallisation) are used than in industry for safety reasons
- **Potassium** is mined as KCl or K_2SO_4
- **Phosphate** rocks (insoluble) are mined and reacted with different acids to produce soluble phosphates (superphosphates)

The Periodic Table of the Elements

1	2											3	4	5	6	7	0
						1 H hydrogen 1											4 He helium 2
7 Li lithium 3	9 Be beryllium 4											11 B boron 5	12 C carbon 6	14 N nitrogen 7	16 O oxygen 8	19 F fluorine 9	20 Ne neon 10
23 Na sodium 11	24 Mg magnesium 12											27 Al aluminium 13	28 Si silicon 14	31 P phosphorus 15	32 S sulfur 16	35.5 Cl chlorine 17	40 Ar argon 18
39 K potassium 19	40 Ca calcium 20	45 Sc scandium 21	48 Ti titanium 22	51 V vanadium 23	52 Cr chromium 24	55 Mn manganese 25	56 Fe iron 26	59 Co cobalt 27	59 Ni nickel 28	63.5 Cu copper 29	65 Zn zinc 30	70 Ga gallium 31	73 Ge germanium 32	75 As arsenic 33	79 Se selenium 34	80 Br bromine 35	84 Kr krypton 36
85 Rb rubidium 37	88 Sr strontium 38	89 Y yttrium 39	91 Zr zirconium 40	93 Nb niobium 41	96 Mo molybdenum 42	[98] Tc technetium 43	101 Ru ruthenium 44	103 Rh rhodium 45	106 Pd palladium 46	108 Ag silver 47	112 Cd cadmium 48	115 In indium 49	119 Sn tin 50	122 Sb antimony 51	128 Te tellurium 52	127 I iodine 53	131 Xe xenon 54
133 Cs caesium 55	137 Ba barium 56	139 La* lanthanum 57	178 Hf hafnium 72	181 Ta tantalum 73	184 W tungsten 74	186 Re rhenium 75	190 Os osmium 76	192 Ir iridium 77	195 Pt platinum 78	197 Au gold 79	201 Hg mercury 80	204 Tl thallium 81	207 Pb lead 82	209 Bi bismuth 83	[209] Po polonium 84	[210] At astatine 85	[222] Rn radon 86
[223] Fr francium 87	[226] Ra radium 88	[227] Ac* actinium 89	[261] Rf rutherfordium 104	[262] Db dubnium 105	[266] Sg seaborgium 106	[264] Bh bohrium 107	[277] Hs hassium 108	[268] Mt meitnerium 109	[271] Ds darmstadtium 110	[272] Rg roentgenium 111							

Key:
relative atomic mass
atomic symbol
name
atomic (proton) number

www.ingramcontent.com/pod-product-compliance
Lightning Source LLC
Chambersburg PA
CBHW051551010526
44118CB00022B/2662